Student Solutions Manual

Financial Accounting for MBAs

Third Edition

Peter D. Easton

John J. Wild

Robert F. Halsey

Mary Lea McAnally

Cambridge

BUSINESS PUBLISHERS

Cambridge Business Publishers

STUDENT SOLUTIONS MANUAL TO ACCOMPANY FINANCIAL ACCOUNTING FOR MBAs, Third Edition, by Peter D. Easton, John J. Wild, Robert F. Halsey, and Mary Lea McAnally.

ISBN 0-9787279-4-0

Printed in the United States of America.
10 9 8 7 6 5 4 3 2 1

CONTENTS

This page is intentionally left blank.

Module 1

Financial Accounting for MBAs

QUESTIONS

Q1-2. An organization's financing activities (liabilities and equity = sources of funds) pay for investing activities (assets = uses of funds). An organization's assets cannot be more or less than its liabilities and equity combined. This means: assets = liabilities + equity. This relation is called the accounting equation (sometimes called the *balance sheet equation*, or BSE), and it applies to all organizations at all times.

Q1-4. The balance sheet provides information that helps users understand a company's resources (assets) and claims to those resources (liabilities and stockholders' equity) as of a given *point in time*.

Q1-6. The statement of cash flows reports on the cash inflows and outflows relating to a company's operating, investing, and financing activities over a period of time. The sum of these three activities yields the net change in cash for the period. This statement is a useful complement to the income statement, which reports on revenues and expenses, but which conveys relatively little information about cash flows.

Q1-8. External users and their uses of accounting information include: (a) lenders for measuring the risk and return of loans; (b) shareholders for assessing the return and risk in acquiring shares; and (c) analysts for assessing investment potential. Other users are auditors, consultants, officers, directors for overseeing management, employees for judging employment opportunities, regulators, unions, suppliers, and appraisers.

Q1-10.[A] Procter & Gamble's independent auditor is Deloitte & Touche LLP. The auditor expressly states that "our responsibility is to express an opinion on these financial statements based on our audits." The auditor also states that "these financial statements are the responsibility of the company's management." Thus, the auditor does not assume responsibility for the financial statements.

Q1-12.[B] Generally Accepted Accounting Principles (GAAP) are the various methods, rules, practices, and other procedures that have evolved over time in response to the need to regulate the preparation of financial statements. They are primarily set by the Financial Accounting Standards Board (FASB), a private sector entity with representatives from companies that issue financial statements, accounting firms that audit those statements, and users of financial information. Other bodies that contribute to GAAP are the AICPA, the EITF, and the SEC.

Q1-14.[B] The auditor's primary function is to express an opinion as to whether the financial statements fairly present the financial condition of the company and are free from material misstatements. Auditors do not prepare the financial statements; they only audit them and issue their opinion on them. The auditors provide no guarantees about the financial statements or about the company's continued performance.

Q1-16. Managers are vitally concerned about disclosing proprietary information that might benefit the company's competitors. Of most concern, is the "cost" of losing some competitive advantage. There has traditionally been tension between companies and the financial professionals (especially investment analysts) who press firms for more and more financial and non-financial information.

Q1-18 Borrowed money must be repaid, both the principal amount borrowed as well as interest on the borrowed funds. These payments have contractual due dates. If payments are not prompt, creditors have powerful legal remedies, including forcing the company into bankruptcy. Consequently, when comparing two companies with the same return on equity, the one using less debt would generally be viewed as a safer (less risky) investment.

MINI EXERCISES

M1-20 (10 minutes)

($ millions)

Assets	=	Liabilities	+	Equity
$315,920		$304,269		$11,651

Ford receives more of its financing from nonowners ($304,269 million) versus owners ($11,651 million). Its owner financing comprises 3.7% of its total financing ($11,651 million/ $315,920 million). The relatively low level of equity capital is primarily the result of the fact that Ford is actually a blend of two companies: the automotive manufacturing company and the financial subsidiary. The financial subsidiary has a balance sheet similar to that of a bank, that is, relatively little equity capital. The blend of these two operating entities results in a balance sheet that is more dependent on borrowed funds than would be the case if Ford consisted solely of the manufacturing company.

M1-22[A] (15 minutes)

In its October, 2006 annual report, Starbucks reports the following figures (in $ millions):

Assets	=	Liabilities	+	Equity
$4,428,941	=	$2,200,435	+	$2,228,506

As shown, the accounting equation holds for Starbucks. Also, we can see that Starbucks's nonowner financing is 50% ($2,200,435 / $4,428,941) of its total financing.

©Cambridge Business Publishers, 2008

M1-24 (20 minutes)

a. BS

b. IS

c. BS

d. BS

e. SCF*

f. BS and SE

g. SCF and SE

h. SCF and SE

i. IS, SE, and SCF

* Reduction of cash and the increase in noncash assets will be reflected in the BS as well, but the cash outflow is a SCF account.

M1-26 [B] (10 minutes)

Internal controls are designed for the following purposes:

- Monitoring an organization's activities to promote efficiency and to prevent wrongful use of its resources
- Ensuring the validity and credibility of external accounting reports
- Promoting effective operations
- Ensuring reliable internal reporting

Congress has a special interest in internal controls and reports about them. Specifically, the absence or failure of internal controls can adversely affect the effectiveness of domestic and global financial markets. Enron provided Congress with a case in point.

EXERCISES

E1-28 (20 minutes)

($ millions)

a. **Using the accounting equation:**

Assets ($44,224)   = Liabilities ($8,756) + Equity (?)

Thus: <u>$35,468</u>   = Equity

b. **Using the accounting equation at the *beginning* of the year:**

Assets ($1,378)   = Liabilities (?) + Equity ($415)

Thus: Beginning Liabilities   = $963

Using the accounting equation at the *end* of the year:

Assets ($1,378 + $70)   = Liabilities ($963 + $30) + Equity (?)

Thus: Ending Equity   = <u>$455</u>

> *Alternative approach to solving part (b):*
> ΔAssets($70) = ΔLiabilities($30) + ΔEquity(?)
> where "Δ" refers to "change in."
>   *Thus:* Δ *Ending* Equity = $70 - $30 = $40 and
>   Ending equity = $415 + $40 = $455

c. **Using the accounting equation at the *end* of the year:**

Assets($50,388)   = Liabilities($26,197 - $100) + Equity(?)

Thus: Ending Equity   = $24,291

Using the accounting equation at the *beginning* of the year:

Assets($50,388 - $400)   Liabilities($26,197) + Equity(?)

Thus: Beginning Equity   = <u>$23,791</u>

E1-30 (10 minutes)

Computation of dividends

Beginning retained earnings, 2005...	$8,223.9
+ Net income	1,351.4
– Cash dividends	(?)
= Ending retained earnings, 2005	$8,968.1

Thus, dividends were $607.2 million for 2005. The company paid out dividends equal to 44.9% of 2005 net income ($607.2 / $1,351.4).

E1-32 (15 minutes)

Return on net operating assets (RNOA) = Net operating profit after tax / Average net operating assets

$$= \$477.2 / [(\$2,777.3 + \$2,973.1)/2]$$

$$= 16.6\%$$

E1-34 (20 minutes)

a. ROE = Net income / Average stockholders' equity
   = $564 million / [($2,229 million + $2,090 million)/2] = 26.1%

b. The repurchase of common stock reduces the denominator (average stockholders' equity). The outflow of cash for the repurchase, however, reduces net income by the return on the cash that is forgone. Generally, the reduction in the denominator is greater than that for the numerator, and consequently ROE increases. That is one of the reasons cited for share repurchases.

c. Companies usually repurchase their own stock when they feel that it is undervalued by the market. The repurchase is a way to send a powerful signal to the market to that effect. Company management is, in essence, backing up its assertions that the stock is undervalued with a tangible investment of the company's funds. Companies also repurchase their own stock to have shares available to give to executives and other employees as compensation.

P1-36 (30 minutes)

General Mills, Inc.
Income Statement ($ millions)
For Year Ended May 30, 2004

Net sales	$11,070
Cost of sales	6,584
Gross profit	4,486
Total expenses	3,431
Net income	$ 1,055

General Mills, Inc.
Balance Sheet ($ millions)
May 30, 2004

Cash & equivalents	$ 751	Total liabilities	$12,901
Noncash assets	17,697	Stockholders' equity	5,547
Total assets	$18,448	Total liabilities and equity	$18,448

General Mills, Inc.
Statement of Cash Flows ($ millions)
For Year Ended May 30, 2004

Net cash provided by operating activities	$ 1,461
Net cash used by investing activities	(470)
Net cash used by financing activities	(943)
Net change in cash	48
Cash, beginning year	703
Cash, ending year	$ 751

P1-38 (30 minutes)

Cisco Systems, Inc.
Income Statement ($ millions)
For Year Ended July 30, 2005

Sales	$24,801
Cost of goods sold	8,130
Gross profit	16,671
Expenses	10,930
Net income	$ 5,741

Cisco Systems, Inc.
Balance Sheet ($ millions)
July 30, 2005

Cash & equivalents	$ 4,742	Total liabilities	$10,699
Noncash assets	29,141	Stockholders' equity	23,184
Total assets	$33,883	Total liabilities and equity	$33,883

Cisco Systems, Inc.
Statement of Cash Flows ($ millions)
For Year Ended July 30, 2005

Cash provided by operating activities	$7,568
Cash provided by investing activities	2,614
Cash used in financing activities	(9,162)
Net change in cash	1,020
Cash, beginning year	3,722
Cash, ending year	$4,742

P1-40 (15 minutes)

EA Systems, Inc. Statement of Stockholders' Equity For Year Ended December 31, 2005			
	Common Stock	Retained Earnings	Stockholders' Equity
December 31, 2004.............................	$ 550	$2,437	$2,987
Net income..		859	859
Cash dividends..................................	_____	(281)	(281)
December 31, 2005.............................	$ 550	$3,015	$3,565

P1-42 (30 minutes)

a. Procter & Gamble is a large company in the highly competitive consumer products sector. Porter's five forces play out as follows for P&G:

- Industry competitors Procter & Gamble has many competitors with similar products that are difficult to differentiate without substantial investment in advertising and promotion. Successful companies in this industry must be able to achieve an optimal balance of product price and advertising expense that maximize profitability. A smaller competitor like KMB may lack pricing power and find it difficult to cover the advertising costs necessary to compete without sacrificing profitability.

- Bargaining power of buyers The footnotes to the 2006 P&G 10-K reveal that 15% of Procter & Gamble's sales are to Wal-Mart. Wal-Mart's size results in considerable buying power that limits seller profits for most companies. Despite P&G's substantial size ($68 billion in revenues), Wal-Mart's buying power ($220 billion cost of goods sold) is formidable. It is likely, therefore, that Wal-Mart exerts a significant level of bargaining power on this segment of P&G sales. Other customers may not be able to exact similar price concessions, however.

- Bargaining power of suppliers P&G is large ($33 billion in cost of goods sold), which implies its suppliers are unlikely to exert forces to significantly increase its cost of sales.

- Threat of substitution Consumer product items are usually not well differentiated, except as a consequence of significant levels of advertising. P&G's advertising expenditures of nearly $7 billion in

2006 are substantial and result in products that typically rank at the top of their sales segments. P&G's advertising budget mitigates the threat of substitution that is typically high in this industry.

- <u>Threat of entry</u> High investment costs to build brand equity are a barrier to entry in P&G's business. Although the costs to introduce a competing product are not significant, the costs to turn that product into a formidable competitor rather than a niche player are significant. Entry is not likely to come from new companies entering the industry. Rather, strong existing competitors with established advertising programs and distribution networks present a more significant threat.

b. Our analysis reveals that P&G is a formidable competitor. Its advertising acumen is legendary and it possesses the financial strength to sustain significant levels of product promotion. Further, the rise in its stock price (50% increase in the past 5 years) provides the company with valuable currency with which to acquire other consumer products companies (i.e., Gillette Company) further strengthening its market position. Our evaluation of P&G's financial statements should consider these dimensions in conjunction with the computation of returns and their components.

P1-44 (20 minutes)

a. RNOA = Net operating profit after tax / Average net operating assets

ANF 2006 RNOA = $352.8 / [($584.0 + $669.3) / 2] = 56.3%

TJX 2006 RNOA = $675.3 / [($2,548.2+$2,321.2)/2] = 27.7%

b.

	ANF	TJX
NOPM	$352.8/$2,784.7 = 12.67%	$675.3/$16,057.9 = 4.21%
NOAT	$2,784.7/[($584.0+$669.3)/2 = 4.44	$16,057.9/[($2,548.2+$2,321.2)/2] = 6.60
RNOA	12.67% x 4.44 = 56.3%	4.21% x 6.60 = 27.8%*

*minor rounding difference from part (a)

c. ANF is an upscale clothing retailer and, thus, premium prices its clothing. This is evident in ANF's higher net operating profit margin (12.67% compared to 4.21% at TJX). TJX's value-pricing business model relies on higher turnover of clothing with lower margins. Although its turnover rate is 50% higher than ANF's, it is not high enough to compensate for its markedly lower net operating profit margin. ANF is performing well on both measures, and its return on net operating assets is more than twice that of TJX.

P1-46 (30 minutes)

a.

	2005	2004	2003
RNOA	$3,256/[($12,209+$12,972)/2]	$2,976/[($12,972+$10,604)/2]	$2,413/[($10,604+$9,132)/2]
	= 25.86%	= 25.25%	= 24.45%

b.

	2005	2004	2003
NOPM	$3,256/$21,167=15.38%	$2,976/$20,011=14.87%	$2,413/$18,232=13.23%
NOAT	$21,167/[($12,209+$12,972)/2]	$20,011/[($12,972+$10,604)/2]	$18,232/[($10,604+$9,132)/2]
	= 1.68	= 1.70	= 1.85
RNOA	15.38% x 1.68 = 25.84%*	14.87% x 1.70 = 25.28%*	13.23% x 1. 85 = 24.48%*

*minor rounding difference from part (a)

c. 3M's RNOA is fairly stable; the slight increase in 2005 compared to 2004 is driven by a slight increase in profitability. NOPM increased from 14.87% in 2004 to 15.38% in 2005. There is a very slight downward trend for net operating asset turnover (NOAT) – the rate declined to 1.70 in 2004 from 1.85 the prior year and, then, decreased slightly again during 2005. The unchanging RNOA is fairly typical for a large company like 3M. Asset turnover rates are stable and any improvement in RNOA typically comes from improved profitability.

P1-48 (20 minutes)

a. Steve Jobs made assertions that the Sarbanes-Oxley Act requires all CEOs and CFOs to make. In particular, Jobs certified that:
   - He has read the financial report.
   - The financial report does not contain any significant (material) misstatement or omit to state a significant fact that should have been included. The financial reports are, therefore, complete.
   - The financial reports fairly present the financial condition of the company.
   - The company maintains a system of internal controls and those controls are functioning correctly.

b. Congress passed the Sarbanes-Oxley Act following a spate of corporate accounting scandals in the early 2000s. The impetus for the legislation was the belief that some CEOs and CFOs no longer assumed responsibility for the financial reporting of their companies. By requiring these high-ranking executives to personally certify to the items referenced in part a above, Congress anticipated closer scrutiny of the financial reporting process at the highest levels of the company.

c. The Sarbanes-Oxley Act prescribes significant penalties for falsely certifying to the completeness and correctness of the financial reports. CEOs and CFOs face fines of up to $5 million and prison terms of up to 20 years. Additionally, should the company later restate its financial statements as a result of wrongful false reporting, the CEOs and CFOs may be required to forfeit any profits earned as a result of that reporting. This forfeiture has been labeled "disgorgement" in the financial press.

CASES

C1-50 (30 minutes)

Financing can come from a number of sources, including operating creditors, borrowed funds, and the sale of stock. Each has its strengths and weaknesses.

1. Operating creditors – operating creditors are merchandise and service suppliers, including employees. Generally, these liabilities are non-interest bearing. As a result, companies typically use this source of credit to the fullest extent possible, often stretching payment times. However, abuse of operating creditors has a significant downside. The company may be unable to supply its operating needs and the damage to employee morale might have significant repercussions. Operating credit must, therefore, be used with care.

2. Borrowed funds – borrowed money typically carries an interest rate. Because interest expense is deductible for tax purposes, borrowed funds reduce income tax expense. The taxes saved are called the "tax shield." The deductibility of interest reduces the effective cost of borrowing. The downside of debt is that the company *must* make principal and interest payments as scheduled. Failure to make payments on time can result in severe consequences – creditors have significant legal remedies, including forcing the company into bankruptcy and requiring its liquidation. The low debt cost must be balanced against the fixed payment obligations.

3. Sale of stock – companies can sell various classes of stock to investors. Some classes of stock have mandatory dividend payments. On other classes of stock, dividends are not a legal requirement until declared by the board of directors. Consequently, unlike debt payments, some dividends can be curtailed in business downturns. The downside of stock issuance is its cost. Because equity is the most expensive source of capital, companies use it sparingly.

C1-52 (30 minutes)

Transparency is the degree to which the financial statements accurately portray the financial condition of the company and the results of its operating activities. Transparent financial statements are timely and provide all the information required to effectively evaluate the financial performance of the company. Accuracy, timeliness and completeness are important to financial statement readers who seek financial information that is relevant and reliable. Transparency became a central issue in financial reporting following the accounting scandals of the early 2000s, when analysts believed too many financial statements lacked transparency.

Balancing companies' desire to issue transparent financial statements is their need to protect proprietary information. Markets are very competitive, and the information disclosed to investors and creditors is also disclosed to the company's competitors. Most critical is information relating to the company's strategic direction. Even historical information, however, provides insight into the relative profitability of the company's operating units that can be effectively utilized by future competitors.

There has traditionally been tension between companies and the financial professionals (especially investment analysts) who press firms for more and more financial and non-financial information.

C1-54^B (30 minutes)

The SEC has voiced its concern over the perceived lack of independence of auditors, and Congress has passed legislation to define the activities that auditors may and may not perform for their clients. The issue of independence first arose when auditors faced no controls. In response to declining audit fees, public accounting firms sought to bolster their income with management consulting engagements, such as tax services, software development, M&A assistance, internal audit outsourcing, supply chain management, and a host of other services.

As management consulting revenues and profits grew disproportionately compared to traditional audit revenues and profit, the SEC became concerned that auditors might be unduly influenced to issue biased audit reports rather than risk losing lucrative management consulting fees from the same client. In response, the SEC compelled public accounting firms to divest their management consulting subsidiaries. Further, firms were limited as the types of non-audit engagements they could perform for clients.

Auditors are an important component of the corporate governance system, and their effectiveness is lessened if their independence is compromised. The board of directors (specifically, the audit committee) must continually evaluate the independence of the company's auditors.

Module 2

Introducing Financial Statements and Transaction Analysis

QUESTIONS

Q2-2. The Revenue Recognition Principle stipulates that revenue should be recorded when it is *earned*. The Matching Principle tells us that expenses should be recorded when they are *incurred*. Neither the recognition of revenue nor the recording of an expense necessarily involves cash. Revenues are recognized first. Then, the expenses incurred in order to generate those revenues are recognized in the same accounting period. That way, profit is correctly reported (e.g., not overstated nor understated).

Q2-4. Transitory items are revenues and expenses that are not expected to recur. The objective of financial analysis is, generally, to predict *future* performance. Given that perspective, transitory (nonrecurring) items are not relevant except to the extent that they convey information about future financial performance.

Q2-6. The Statement of Cash Flows reports the company's cash inflows and outflows during the period, and categorizes them according to operating, investing and financing activities. The income statement reports profit earned under accrual accounting, but does not provide sufficient information concerning cash flows. The Statement of Cash Flows fills that void.

Q2-8. When a company purchases a machine it records the cost as an asset since it will provide future benefits. As the machine is used up, a portion of this cost is transferred from the balance sheet to the income statement as depreciation expense. The machine asset is, thus, reduced by the accumulated depreciation and Equity is reduced as the expense reduces net income and Retained Earnings. This is the Matching Principle. It is critical to the proper recognition of profit. If the entire cost of the machine was immediately expensed, profit would be reduced considerably in the year the machine was purchased. Then, in subsequent years, net income would be far too high as none of the machine's cost would be matched against the revenues it generates in those years.

Q2-10. Liquidity refers to the ready availability of cash. That is, how much cash the company has on hand, how much cash is being generated, and how much cash can be raised quickly. Liquidity is essential to the survival of the business. After all, firms must pay loans and employee wages with cash.

Q2-12. GAAP uses historical costs because they are less subjective than market values. Market values can be biased for two reasons: first, we may not be able to measure them accurately (consider our inability to accurately measure the market value of a manufacturing facility, for example), and second, managers may intervene in the reporting process to intentionally bias the results in order to achieve a particular objective (like enhancing the stock price).

Q2-14. An intangible asset is an asset that that is not physical in nature. To be included on the balance sheet, it has to meet two tests: the company owns the asset, and it will provide future economic benefits. Some examples are goodwill, patents and trademarks, contractual agreements like royalties, leases, and franchise agreements. An intangible asset is only recorded on the balance sheet when it is purchased from an outside party. For example, goodwill arises when the company pays (cash or stock) to acquire another company's brand name or any of the other intangibles listed above.

Q2-16. Net working capital = current assets – current liabilities. Increasing the amount of trade credit (e.g., accounts payable to suppliers) increases current liabilities and reduces net working capital. Trade credit is like borrowing from a supplier to make purchases. As trade credit increases, the supplier is lending more money than before. This frees up cash and thus, net working capital decreases. This can be a good thing. As a business grows, its net working capital grows because inventories and receivables generally grow faster than accounts payable and accrued liabilities do. Net working capital must be financed just like long-term assets.

Q2-18. The arrow running from net income to earned capital in the transaction analysis template denotes that retained earnings (part of earned capital) have been updated to record the profit earned during the period. Retained earnings are reconciled as follows: beginning retained earnings + profit (– loss) – dividends = ending retained earnings. The line, thus, represents the profits that have been added (or the losses subtracted) in calculating an updated balance in the retained earnings account (dividends are recorded as a direct reduction of retained earnings in the template).

MINI EXERCISES

M2-20 (15 minutes)

a.   Balance sheet

b.   Income statement

c.   Balance sheet

d.   Income statement

e.   Balance sheet

f.   Balance sheet

g.   Balance sheet

h.   Balance sheet

i.   Income statement

j.   Income statement

k.   Balance sheet

l.   Balance sheet

M2-22 (15 minutes)

a.   A

b.   L

c.   E

d.   A

e.   L

f.   E

g.   E

h.   L

M2-24 (10 minutes)

Johnson & Johnson Statement of Retained Earnings For Year Ended January 1, 2006	
Retained earnings, January 2, 2005	$35,223
Add: Net income	10,411
Less: Dividends	(3,793)
Other retained earnings changes	(370)
Retained earnings, January 1, 2006	$41,471

M2-26 (15 minutes)

		Balance Sheet					Income Statement		
Transaction	Cash Asset	+ Noncash Assets	= Liabil-ities	+ Contrib. Capital	+ Earned Capital	Rev-enues	− Expen-ses	= Net Income

Cash   1,000
   CS   1,000

Cash
1,000	

CS
	1,000

a. Issue stock for $1,000 cash
- Cash Asset: +1,000 Cash
- Contrib. Capital: +1,000 Common Stock
- Revenues: −
- Net Income: =

INV   500
   Cash   500

INV
500	

Cash
	500

b. Purchase inventory for $500 cash
- Cash Asset: −500 Cash
- Noncash Assets: +500 Inventory
- Revenues: −
- Net Income: =

AR   2,000
   Sales   2,000
COGS   500
   INV   500

AR
2,000	

Sales
	2,000

COGS
500	

INV
	500

c. Sell inventory for $2,000 on account
- Noncash Assets: +2,000 Accounts Receivable; −500 Inventory
- Earned Capital: +1,500 Retained Earnings
- Revenues: +2,000 Sales
- Expenses: +500 Cost of Goods Sold
- Net Income: = +1,500

Cash   2,000
   AR   2,000

Cash
2,000	

AR
	2,000

d. Collect $2,000 on account receivable
- Cash Asset: +2,000 Cash
- Noncash Assets: −2,000 Accounts Receivable
- Revenues: −
- Net Income: =

EXERCISES

E2-28 (15 minutes)

Baiman Corporation Income Statement For Month ended January 31	
Sales..............................	$30,000
Wage expense	12,000
Net income (loss)	$18,000

Baiman Corporation Balance Sheet January	
Cash	$ 0
Accounts receivable	30,000
Total assets	$30,000
Wages payable	$12,000
Retained earnings......................	18,000
Total liabilities and equity	$30,000

E2-30 (15 minutes)

		Balance Sheet					Income Statement		
	Transaction	Cash Asset	+ Noncash Assets	= Liabil-ities	+ Contrib. Capital	+ Earned Capital	Rev-enues	− Expen-ses	= Net Income
Cash 100,000 PPE 20,000 CS 120,000 Cash 100,000 | PPE 20,000 |	a. Issued stock for $100,000 cash and PPE of $20,000.	+100,000 Cash	+20,000 PPE =		+120,000 Common Stock			−	=
CS | 120,000 RNE 3,200 Cash 3,200 RNE 3,200 | Cash | 3,200	b. Paid $3,200 for rent.	-3,200 Cash		=		-3,200 Retained Earnings		+3,200 Rent Expense −	= -3,200
Cash 4,000 Rev 4,000 Cash 4,000 | Rev | 4,000	c. Performed services for $4,000 cash.	+4,000 Cash		=		+4,000 Retained Earnings	+4,000 Revenue	−	= +4,000

AR   14,000
  Rev   14,000

d.

AR	
14,000	

Rev	
	14,000

Performed services for $14,000 on account.

+14,000 Accounts Receivable = +14,000 Retained Earnings | +14,000 Revenue − = +14,000

WE   4,800
  Cash   4,800

e. Paid $4,800 cash for wages.

WE	
4,800	

Cash	
	4,800

−4,800 Cash = −4,800 Retained Earnings | − +4,800 Wages Expense = −4,800

Cash   10,000
  AR   10,000

f. Received $10,000 cash on receivable.

Cash	
10,000	

AR	
	10,000

+10,000 Cash −10,000 Accounts Receivable = | − =

DIV   935
  Cash   935

g. Paid dividends of $935.

DIV	
935	

Cash	
	935

−935 Cash = −935 Retained Earnings | − =

E2-32 (15 minutes)

a.

Target Corp ($ millions)	Amount	Classification
Sales	$ 48,163	I
Accumulated depreciation	6,178	B
Depreciation expense	1,320	I
Retained earnings	9,648	B
Net income	1,841	I
Property, plant & equipment	16,969	B
Selling, general & admin expense	11,534	I
Accounts receivable	5,776	B
Total liabilities	20,327	B
Stockholders' equity	$ 11,065	B

b. Total Assets = Total Liabilities + Stockholders' Equity
   Total Assets = $20,327 + $11,065 = $31,392

   Total Revenue – Total Expenses = Net Income
   $48,163 – Total Expenses = $1,841

   Thus, Total Expenses = $46,322

c. Net Profit Margin = Net income / Sales
   Net Profit Margin = $1,841 / $48,163 = 3.82%

   Total Liabilities -to-Equity Ratio = Total Liabilities / Stockholders' Equity
   Total Liabilities -to-Equity Ratio = $20,327 / $11,065 = 1.84

E2-34 (15 minutes)

a.

	AAPL		DELL	
Sales	$13,931		$49,205	
COGS	9,888	71.0%	40,190	81.7%
Gross profit	4,043	29.0%	9,015	18.3%
Total expenses	2,708	19.4%	5,972	12.1%
Net income	$ 1,335	9.6%	$ 3,043	6.2%

AAPL's gross profit margin is more than 50% greater than DELL's. This is likely due to two factors: first, a significant proportion of AAPL's sales relate to the iPod, a very high-margin product. Second, DELL competes as the low price leader in the PC-sales segment.

b.

	AAPL		DELL	
Current assets	$10,300	89.2%	$16,897	72.8%
Long-term assets	1,251	10.8%	6,318	27.2%
Total assets	$11,551		$23,215	
Current liabilities	$ 3,484	30.2%	$14,136	60.9%
Long-term liabilities	601	5.2%	2,594	11.2%
Total liabilities	4,085	35.4%	16,730	72.1%
Stockholders' equity	7,466	64.6%	6,485	27.9%
Total liabs and equity	$11,551		$23,215	

AAPL has a greater proportion of stockholders' equity in its capital structure. Neither of these companies carries a significant percentage of long-term debt. A greater proportion of debt is generally viewed as a riskier capital structure. However, DELL's relatively high level of short-term debt arises from the fact that the company relies very heavily on supplier financing. DELL is a significant customer for many of its suppliers, which gives Dell bargaining power over credit terms. DELL's high level of profitability also lessens any concerns one might have regarding its solvency. AAPL's equity growth has been recent, resulting from the meteoric rise of the highly profitable iPod. Unless the company has need for this level of capital (and the cash that has stockpiled as a result), it may come under pressure to pay some of its accumulated cash out to shareholders in the form of a dividend or stock repurchase.

E2-36 (30 minutes)

a.

	TJX		VZ	
Sales	$14,913		$75,112	
COGS	11,399	76.4%	25,469	33.9%
Gross profit	3,514	23.6%	49,643	66.1%
Total expenses	2,904	19.5%	42,246	56.2%
Net income	$ 610	4.1%	$ 7,397	9.8%

TJX is a value-priced clothing retailer whose main expense is cost of sales. VZ operates in the highly capital intensive telecom industry. The difference in their respective business models is clearly evident in the level of gross profit and operating expenses. VZ's gross profit margin is over 2.5 times that of TJX. This does not imply that VZ is a better managed company. VZ's industry is very capital intensive, and the industry requires a significant level of gross profit in order to cover its higher level of operating expenses, the most significant of which is depreciation expense related to its long-term assets. VZ net income as a percentage of sales is more than twice that of TJX. On this dimension, VZ's business model appears to be more profitable.

b.

	TJX	VZ
Sales	$14,913	$ 75,112
Total assets	$ 5,075	$168,130
Sales / total assets	2.94	0.45

TJX's sales are almost three times its total assets. VZ's sales are less than half of total assets. This metric clearly demonstrates the capital intensity of

VZ's industry and the fact that TJX turns over its inventory (the major asset) many times a year.

c.

	TJX	VZ
Total liabilities	$3,328	$101,696
Stockholders' equity......................................	$1,747	$ 66,434
Total liabilities / Stockholders' equity........	1.90	1.53

Both companies have more debt than equity although TJX has proportionately more. Companies with higher proportions of debt are generally viewed as riskier because failure to make required debt payments can have significant negative consequences.

d.

VZ's debt level is a potential problem area given the significant capital expenditures that will be required in order to upgrade its infrastructure to remain competitive. Substituting higher cost equity capital, though ameliorating concerns about debt payment, will reduce return on equity. At TJX, inventory turns over quickly, which increases the likelihood that the company will have cash to pay off current liabilities as they come due.

e.

	TJX	VZ
Net income...	$ 610	$ 7,397
Stockholders' equity.................................	$1,747	$66,434
Net income / Stockholders' equity	34.9%	11.1%

TJX net income to stockholders' equity ratio (ROE) is more than three times that of VZ. Although TJX's profit per sales dollar is half that of VZ, its sales-to-assets ratio more than offsets the difference. TJX relies on asset productivity to drive its returns, and appears to be succeeding on that dimension. Further, it is able to minimize its equity capital investment by substituting debt. On balance, the TJX business model appears to be the more successful of the two. Side note: the market value of TJX is 5.9 times the book value per share as of December, 2005, compared with 2.4 times for VZ.

PROBLEMS

P2-38 (30 minutes)

a.

3M	Current Assets	Long-term Assets	Total Assets	Current Liabilities	Long-term Liabilities	Total Liabilities	Stockholders' Equity
2001	$6,296	$8,310	$14,606	$4,509	$4,011	$8,520	$6,086
2002	6,059	9,270	15,329	4,457	4,879	9,336	5,993
2003	7,720	9,880	17,600	5,082	4,633	9,715	7,885
2004	8,720	11,988	20,708	6,071	4,259	10,330	10,378
2005	7,115	13,398	20,513	5,238	5,175	10,413	10,100

b. 3M's current assets most likely include cash, accounts receivable, inventories, and prepaid assets.

Its long-term assets most likely include property, plant and equipment (PPE), goodwill, and other intangible assets that have arisen from acquisitions.

P2-40 (30 minutes)

a.

Albertsons Inc.	Current Assets	Long-term Assets	Total Assets	Current Liabilities	Long-term Liabilities	Total Liabilities	Stockholders' Equity
2002	$4,609	$11,358	$15,967	$3,582	$6,470	$10,052	$5,915
2003	4,268	10,943	15,211	3,448	6,566	10,014	5,197
2004	4,419	10,975	15,394	3,685	6,328	10,013	5,381
2005	4,295	14,016	18,311	4,085	8,805	12,890	5,421
2006	4,355	13,516	17,871	3,880	8,284	12,164	5,707

b. For a grocery chain like Albertsons, it would seem reasonable that inventories and cash would be the predominant current assets. Grocery stores don't sell on credit, so accounts receivable would be minimal. In reality, inventories are not a large dollar amount because the company's business model depends on high inventory turnover—that is, it works diligently to minimize inventory levels in a push for freshness. Long-term assets are primarily concentrated in property, plant and equipment (PPE), that is, the stores, the cash registers, the shelving and freezers.

©Cambridge Business Publishers, 2008

c. No, the company is not conservatively financed. Albertsons' stockholders' equity represents 32% of its total capitalization – computed as $5,707 / ($12,164 + $5,707). Although its dependence on debt financing is not extreme, its equity capital does not represent a large proportion of total capitalization relative to other grocery companies.

P2-42 (30 minutes)

a.

Company	Net Income / Sales	Rank
Federated Dept. Stores	6.3%	2
Home Depot Inc.	7.2%	1
Staples Inc.	5.2%	3
Target Corp.	4.6%	4
Wal-Mart Stores	3.6%	5

Home Depot and Federated Dept. Stores report the highest net profit margins. These companies have succeeded at differentiating their brands. Wal-Mart competes on price in an undifferentiated market space. Although Staples and Target do not compete on price alone, they are in highly competitive markets with undifferentiated product lines.

b.

Company	Operating Cash Flow / Sales	Rank
Federated Dept. Stores	8.7%	1
Home Depot Inc.	8.0%	3
Staples Inc.	7.7%	4
Target Corp.	8.5%	2
Wal-Mart Stores	5.6%	5

The ranking does not correspond to the profit margin ranking in part a. While Target, Home Depot and Federated are very similar on the operating cash flow dimension, they have vastly different profitability ratios. The only common ranking is Wal-Mart that ranks last on both lists. These different rankings highlight the fact that profitability (measured with GAAP) can differ significantly from operating cash flows – the two are very different concepts.

c.

Company	Investing Cash Flow / Sales	Rank
Federated Dept. Stores	-11.2%	1
Home Depot Inc.	-5.6%	3
Staples Inc.	-3.9%	5
Target Corp.	-7.9%	2
Wal-Mart Stores	-4.5%	4

With the exception of Staples and Wal-Mart that switch places in the ranking, the cash flows related to investing activities coincide with the operating cash flow rankings. This implies that companies that made more cash from operations, used more cash to expand and invest. This means that these companies are growing.

d. Negative cash flows from financing activities can occur for three reasons: debt repayments (in excess of new borrowings), stock repurchases (in excess of stock sales), and dividend payments. Companies typically do not reduce debt unless their debt levels are uncomfortably high or the company has excess cash or marketable securities. Companies repurchase their stock in order to 1) signal to the market that the company believes its stock is undervalued, 2) to return capital to shareholders in a tax-advantaged way (e.g., if the tax rates on capital gains are less than those on dividends), or 3) to honor employee stock option exercises. Not all companies pay dividends so this is not as common as the first two reasons for negative financing cash flows.

P2-44 (40 minutes)

a. Depreciation is added back to undo the effect it had on the income statement. Verizon deducted $14,047 depreciation in computing net income. Depreciation is a non-cash expense so Verizon did not actually use $14,047 cash to pay depreciation. Thus, to determine how much cash was generated, net income is too low by the depreciation amount of $14,047. The depreciation add-back is <u>NOT</u> a source of cash as some mistakenly believe. Cash is, ultimately, generated by profitable operations, not by depreciation.

b. The depreciation add-back is twice the level of net income. This signifies a highly capital-intensive industry.

c. The MD&A section of the 10-K provides management's assessment of the operating results and investment activities of the company. This is a source of useful information that includes less promotion material than other statements by the company since it is regulated by SEC disclosure rules.

d. Repaying long-term debt with short-term notes is cause for concern, as this activity does nothing to alleviate the short term demands for cash. Refinancing with longer term debt would address liquidity concerns. On the other hand, short-term rates are typically lower than long-term rates and refinancing might save some interest expense. However, in 2005 interest rates were climbing so repaying older, lower-rate debt with newer higher-rate debt seems counterproductive.

e. Dividends are not a contractual obligation until declared by the board of directors. Although stock price may fall if the company reduces dividends, shareholders cannot force the company into bankruptcy like debt holders can. Dividends differ significantly from debt.

f. Verizon's operations generated a significant amount of cash. Its capital expenditures are significant as the company continues to upgrade its infrastructure to implement new technology to remain competitive with other telecom and cable companies. High capital outlays would, ordinarily, not be a problem were it not for the company's significant existing debt load. Verizon's debt repayment obligation for 2005 was nearly $4 billion, in addition to the interest expense that is recorded in its income statement. Although the company is financial strong, balancing its debt level with the cash flow needs for capital expenditures to support its operating activities and dividends to support its stock price is a difficult challenge facing the company.

P2-46 (20 minutes)

AniFoods, Inc. Income Statement For Month Ended March 31	
Sales...	$100,000
Cost of goods sold...	(70,000)
Gross profit..	30,000
Advertising expense...	(7,500)
Wages expense..	(16,000)
Depreciation expense...	(2,000)
Net income...	$ 4,500

AniFoods, Inc. Balance Sheet March 31			
Cash..............................	$100,000	Wages payable........................	$ 1,000
Accounts receivable......	40,000	Note payable (to owner).............	55,000
Inventory.......................	10,000	Note payable (to vendor)............	40,000
Prepaid advertising.......	2,500	Total liabilities........................	96,000
Equipment, gross...........	50,000		
Accumulated dep'n........	(2,000)	Common stock........................	100,000
Equipment, net..............	48,000	Retained earnings...................	4,500
Total assets...................	$200,500	Total liabilities and equity......	$200,500

C2-48 (25 minutes)

a. The cash cycle is the number of days that pass from the time the company pays cash to purchase or manufacture inventory, sells the inventory and ultimately collects the accounts receivable. This period of time is reduced to the extent that suppliers finance a portion of the inventory purchase.

Receivables and inventories are costly to maintain. They must be financed (either with borrowed funds or by forgoing investment in other earning assets), collected (with some prospect of loss), stored, insured, and moved. By reducing the amount of investment in these assets, companies can reduce their expenses and their need for external capital.

b. A company might reduce its cash cycle by reducing receivables and inventories and by increasing accounts payable.

1. Receivables – receivables can be reduced by invoking more stringent credit-granting policies and faster collection. Companies need appropriate policies to decide to whom to extend credit and in what dollar amount. As credit policies become more restrictive, the dollar amount of receivables declines.

2. Inventories – for retailers, inventories are the cost of the goods purchased for resale. For manufacturers, inventory costs include raw materials, and additional labor and overhead costs to convert the goods into salable form. Reducing the quantities of inventories on hand will reduce the cash cycle time. This can happen with more efficient buying (purchasing for actual orders rather than for estimated demand) and with leaner manufacturing processes.

3. Payables – lengthening the time to pay accounts payable ("leaning on the trade") reduces the cash cycle time as less of the company's own capital is invested in receivables and inventories.

C2-48—continued.

c. Each action described above has implications for the company's relations with customers and suppliers.

1. Receivables – receivables are a marketing tool, like advertising, product promotions and selling expenses. Tightening a company's credit policies can adversely affect sales. On the other hand, more restrictive credit policies can reduce collection costs, bad debt expense and financing costs. Establishing a credit policy and the attendant collection procedures, involves balancing the competing effects of lost sales with cost savings.

2. Inventories – reducing finished goods inventory levels increases the risk of stock-outs and could result in lost sales. The decision about what depth and breadth of finished goods inventories to carry is as much a marketing decision as it is a financial one. Further the amount of raw materials and work-in-process inventories on hand affects production efficiency and has financial implications. Inventory management is a delicate process that must be handled with care to balance competing needs.

3. Payables – lengthening the time to pay accounts payable, while reducing the cash cycle, may also damage relations with suppliers. One company's account payable is another's account receivable. There is a natural tension between two companies seeking to balance the period of time that the credit is outstanding. Although extending payables is favorable from a financial viewpoint, should supplier relations become strained, the company's ability to obtain additional products or services may be jeopardized. Policies relating to the payment of suppliers must be handled with care.

Working capital management is as much art as it is science. Companies must consider many constituencies in framing the appropriate policies.

©Cambridge Business Publishers, 2008

Module 3

Constructing Financial Statements and Analyzing Transactions

QUESTIONS

Q3-2 A journal entry records a transaction in a company's "general journal." A general journal is a book of original entry for the initial recording of any type of transaction or accrual. It contains space for dates and for accounts to be debited and credited, columns for the amounts of the debits and credits, and a posting reference column for numbers of the accounts that are posted. Most companies have electronic journals but the basics are the same.

Q3-4 1. Prepaid Expenses – Allocating assets to expense to reflect expenses incurred during the period. *Example:* Recording supplies used by debiting Supplies Expense and crediting Supplies or recording depreciation expense and reducing PPE (or increasing accumulated depreciation).

2. Unearned Revenues – Adjusting unearned revenues to reflect revenues earned during the period. *Example:* Recording service fees earned by debiting Unearned Service Fees and crediting Service Fees Earned.

3. Accrued Expenses – Accruing expenses to reflect expenses incurred during the period that are not yet paid or recorded. *Example:* Recording unpaid wages by debiting Wages Expense and crediting Wages Payable or recording interest owing on loans.

4. Accrued Revenues – Accruing revenues to reflect revenues earned during the period that are not yet received or invoiced. *Example:* Recording commissions earned by debiting Commissions Receivable and crediting Commissions Earned.

Q3-6 (a) Supplies Expense of $455 must be recorded for the period. This will reduce the asset account and increase the expense account by $455. ($825+$260-$630=$455)

(b) If the adjustment is not made, Supplies Expense is understated by $455, Supplies (asset) and Equity are both overstated by $455 on the January 31 balance sheet.

Q3-8 (a) Jan. 1 Cash.. 9,720

Subscriptions Received in Advance 9,720

To record receipt of two-year subscriptions.

(b) Jan. 31 Subscriptions Received in Advance............................. 405

Subscriptions Revenue 405

To record subscription revenue earned during January ($9,720 / 24 = $405).

Q3-10 On January 31, the interest receivable account and the interest income account both should be increased by $360 to reflect the fact that the company has earned interest but not yet received it.

The journal entry would be as follows:

Jan. 31 Interest Receivable... 360

Interest Income 360

To record interest earned during January.

MINI EXERCISES

M3-12 (20 minutes)

		Balance Sheet					Income Statement		
	Transaction	Cash Asset	+ Noncash Assets	= Liabil- ities	+ Contrib. Capital	+ Earned Capital	Rev- enues	− Expen- ses	= Net Income
Cash 12,000 CS 12,000 Cash 12,000 | CS | 12,000	June 1. Invested $12,000 cash	+12,000 Cash		=	+12,000 Common Stock				
RNE 950 Cash 950 RNE 950 | Cash | 950	June 2. Paid $950 cash for June rent	-950 Cash		=		-950 Retained Earnings		+950 Rent Expense	= -950
PPE 6,400 AP 6,400 PPE 6,400 | AP | 6,400	June 3. Purchased $6,400 of office equipment on credit		+6,400 Office Equipment	= +6,400 Accounts Payable					
SUP 3,800 Cash 1,800 AP 2,000 SUP 3,800 | Cash | 1,800 AP | 2,000	June 6. Purchased $3,800 of supplies; $1,800 cash, $2,000 on account	-1,800 Cash	+3,800 Supplies	= +2,000 Accounts Payable					
AR 4,700 Rev 4,700 AR 4,700 | Rev | 4,700	June 11. $4,700 billed for services		+4,700 Accounts Receivable	=		+4,700 Retained Earnings	+4,700 Service Fees Earned (Revenue)	−	= +4,700

M3-12—continued.

		Balance Sheet						Income Statement		
	Transaction	Cash Asset	+ Noncash Assets	= Liabil-ities	+ Contrib Capital	+ Earned Capital	Rev-enues	− Expen-ses	= Net Income

Cash 3,250 AR 3,250 Cash 3,250 | AR | 3,250	June 17. Collect $3,250 on accounts	+3,250 Cash	-3,250 Accounts Receivable	=					
AP 3,000 Cash 3,000 AP 3,000 | Cash | 3,000	June 19. Paid $3,000 on office equipment account	-3,000 Cash		= -3,000 Accounts Payable					
RE 900 Cash 900 RE 900 | Cash | 900	June 25. Paid cash dividend of $900	-900 Cash		=		-900 Retained Earnings			
UE 350 Cash 350 UE 350 | Cash | 350	June 30. Paid $350 utilities	-350 Cash		=		-350 Retained Earnings		+350 − Utility expense	= -350
WE 2,500 Cash 2,500 WE 2,500 | Cash | 2,500	June 30. Paid $2,500 salaries	-2,500 Cash		=		-2,500 Retained Earnings		+2,500 − Wages expense	= -2,500

M3-14 (40 minutes)

		Balance Sheet					Income Statement		
	Transaction	Cash Asset	+ Noncash Assets	= Liabil-ities	+ Contrib Capital	+ Earned Capital	Rev-enues	− Expen-ses	= Net Income
Cash 9,000 CS 9,000 Cash 9,000| CS |9,000	April 1. Invested $9,000 in cash	+9,000 Cash		=	+9,000 Common Stock				=
PPRNT 2,850 Cash 2,850 PPRNT 2,850| Cash |2,850	April 2. Paid $2,850 cash for lease	-2,850 Cash	+2,850 Prepaid Van Lease	=					=
Cash 10,000 NP 10,000 Cash 10,000| NP |10,000	April 3. Borrow $10,000	+10,000 Cash		= +10,000 Note Payable					=
PPE 5,500 Cash 2,500 AP 3,000 PPE 5,500| Cash |2,500 AP |3,000	April 4. Purchase $5,500 equipment for $2,500 cash with rest on account	-2,500 Cash	+5,500 Equipment	= +3,000 Accounts Payable					=
SUP 4,300 Cash 4,300 SUP 4,300| Cash |4,300	April 5. Paid $4,300 cash for supplies	-4,300 Cash	+4,300 Supplies	=					=

Student Solutions Manual, Module 3

M3-14—Continued

AE   350
  Cash   350

AE
350	

Cash
	350

April 7. Paid $350 cash for ad.

-350 Cash   =   -350 Retained Earnings   +350 − Advertising Expense = -350

AR   3,500
  Rev   3,500

AR
3,500	

Rev
	3,500

April 21. Billed $3,500 for services

+3,500 Accounts Receivable = +3,500 Retained Earnings   +3,500 Cleaning Fees Earned (Revenue) − = +3,500

AP   3,000
  Cash   3,000

AP
3,000	

Cash
	3,000

April 23. Paid $3,000 cash on account

-3,000 Cash = -3,000 Accounts Payable   − =

Cash   2,300
  AR   2,300

Cash
2,300	

AR
	2,300

April 28. Collect $2,300 on account

+2,300 Cash -2,300 Accounts Receivable =   − =

RE   1,000
  Cash   1,000

RE
1,000	

Cash
	1,000

April 29. Paid $1,000 cash dividend

-1,000 Cash = -1,000 Retained Earnings   − =

WE   1,750
  Cash   1,750

WE
1,750	

Cash
	1,750

April 30. Paid $1,750 cash for salaries

-1,750 Cash = -1,750 Retained Earnings   +1,750 − Wages Expense = -1,750

OE   995
  Cash   995

OE
995	

Cash
	995

April 30. Paid $995 cash for gas

-995 Cash = -995 Retained Earnings   +995 − Van Fuel (Operating) Expense = -995

M3-16 (10 minutes)

a.

	Balance Sheet					Income Statement		
Transaction	Cash Asset	+ Noncash Assets	= Liabil- ities	+ Contrib Capital	+ Earned Capital	Rev- enues	− Expen- ses	= Net Income
Received $20,100 in advance for contract work	+20,100 Cash				+20,100 = Unearned Revenue			

Cash 20,100
  UR 20,100

Cash	
20,100	

UR	
	20,100

b.

	Balance Sheet					Income Statement		
Transaction	Cash Asset	+ Noncash Assets	= Liabil- ities	+ Contrib Capital	+ Earned Capita	Rev- enues	− Expen- ses	= Net Income
Adjusting entry for work completed by Jan. 31*			−3,350 = Unearned Revenue			+3,350 Revenue	−	= +3,350

UR 3,350
  Rev 3,350

UR	
3,350	

Rev	
	3,350

* $20,100/6 = $3,350

c.

	Balance Sheet					Income Statement		
Transaction	Cash Asset	+ Noncash Assets	= Liabil- ities	+ Contrib Capital	+ Earned Capital	Rev- enues	− Expen- ses	= Net Income
Adjusting entry for fees earned but not billed		+570 Fees Receivable	=		+570 Retained Earnings	+570 Service Revenue	−	= +570

AR 570
  Rev 570

AR	
570	

Rev	
	570

M3-18 (25 minutes)

a.

IE 185
 PPI 185

	IE	
185		

	PPI	
	185	

	Balance Sheet					Income Statement		
Transaction	Cash Asset	+ Noncash Assets	= Liabil-ities	+ Contrib Capital	+ Earned Capital	Rev-enues	− Expen-ses	= Net Income
Adjusting entry for prepaid insurance	-185 Prepaid Insurance	=			-185 Retained Earnings		+185 − Insurance Expense	= -185

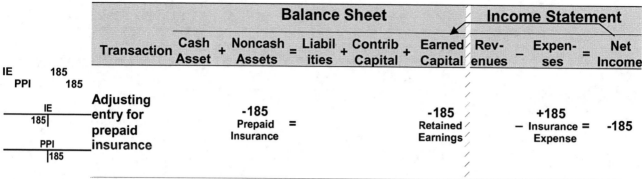

b.

SUPE 1,080
 SUP 1,080

	SUPE	
1,080		

	SUP	
	1,080	

	Balance Sheet					Income Statement		
Transaction	Cash Asset	+ Noncash Assets	= Liabil-ities	+ Contrib Capital	+ Earned Capital	Rev-enues	− Expen-ses	= Net Income
Adjusting entry for supplies used	-1,080 Supplies	=			-1,080 Retained Earnings		+1,080 − Supplies Expense	= -1,080

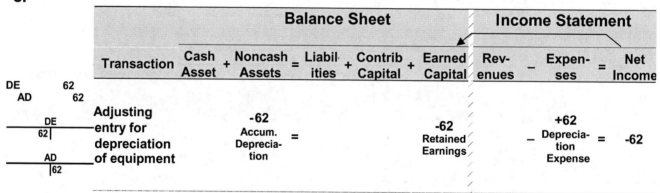

c.

DE 62
 AD 62

	DE	
62		

	AD	
	62	

	Balance Sheet					Income Statement		
Transaction	Cash Asset	+ Noncash Assets	= Liabil-ities	+ Contrib Capital	+ Earned Capital	Rev-enues	− Expen-ses	= Net Income
Adjusting entry for depreciation of equipment	-62 Accum. Deprecia-tion	=			-62 Retained Earnings		+62 − Deprecia-tion Expense	= -62

d.

	Balance Sheet					Income Statement		
Transaction	Cash Asset	+ Noncash Assets	= Liabil-ities	+ Contrib Capital	+ Earned Capital	Rev-enues	− Expen-ses	= Net Income
Adjusting entry for rent revenue earned			-875 = Unearned Rent Revenue		+875 Retained Earnings	+875 Rent Revenue	−	= +875

UR 875
  Rev 875

UR	
875	

	Rev
	875

e.

	Balance Sheet					Income Statement		
Transaction	Cash Asset	+ Noncash Assets	= Liabil-ities	+ Contrib Capital	+ Earned Capital	Rev-enues	− Expen-ses	= Net Income
Adjusting entry for accrued salaries			+490 = Wages Payable		-490 Retained Earnings		− +490 Wages Expense	= -490

WE 490
  WP 490

WE	
490	

	WP
	490

M3-20 (25 minutes)

a.

	Balance Sheet					Income Statement		
Transaction	Cash Asset	+ Noncash Assets	= Liabil-ities	+ Contrib Capital	+ Earned Capita	Rev-enues	− Expen-ses	= Net Income
Inventory purchases (total)		+4,047 Inventory	= +4,047 Accounts Payable				−	=

INV 4,047
  AP 4,047

INV	
4,047	

	AP
	4,047

b. $381 + 4,047 − $361 = Payments = $4,067. This is the amount in cash payments derived using the information in the accounts payable account.

M3-20—concluded

c.

		Balance Sheet					Income Statement		
Transaction	Cash Asset	+ Noncash Assets	= Liabil- ities	+ Contrib Capital	+ Earned Capital	Rev- enues	− Expen- ses	= Net Income
Adjusting entry for cost of goods sold for 2004*		−3,944 Inventory	=			−3,944 Retained Earnings		− +3,944 COGS	= −3,944

```
COGS   3,944
  INV      3,944

   COGS
  3,944|

    INV
       |3,944
```

* $1,151 + $4,047 − $1,254 = COGS = $3,944

M3-22 (15 minutes)

Leuz Architect Services Statement of Stockholders' Equity For Year Ended December 31, 2006			
	Common Stock	Retained Earnings	Total Stockholders' Equity
Balance at December 31, 2005	$30,000	$18,000	$48,000
Stock issuance	6,000		6,000
Dividends		(9,700)	(9,700)
Net income		29,900	29,900
Balance at December 31, 2006	$36,000	$38,200	$74,200

M3-24 (20 minutes)

a.

		Balance Sheet					Income Statement		
Transaction	Cash Asset	+ Noncash Assets	= Liabil- ities	+ Contrib Capital	+ Earned Capital	Rev- enues	− Expen- ses	= Net Income

INV 29,238
  AP   29,238

INV									
29,238									

Transaction	Cash Asset	+ Noncash Assets	= Liabil- ities	+ Contrib Capital	+ Earned Capital	Rev- enues	− Expen- ses	= Net Income
Purchase of inventory on account		+29,238 Inventory	= +29,238 Accounts Payable				−	=

AP
     |29,238

b. Payments to suppliers during the year totaled $29,101. This is calculated using the accounts payable balances and the purchases from part a. as follows: $2,695 + $29,238 - $2,832 = $29,101.

c.

		Balance Sheet					Income Statement		

COGS 28,443
  INV   28,443

COGS									
28,443									

Transaction	Cash Asset	+ Noncash Assets	= Liabil- ities	+ Contrib Capital	+ Earned Capital	Rev- enues	− Expen- ses	= Net Income
Recognize cost of goods sold		-28,443 Inventory	=		-28,443 Retained Earnings		− +28,443 COGS	= -28,443

INV
     |28,443

*We calculate COGS using the information in the inventory account and the purchases, given. $5,911 + $29,238 - $6,706 = $28,443.

EXERCISES

E3-26 (30 minutes)

		Balance Sheet					Income Statement		
	Transaction	Cash Asset	+ Noncash Assets	= Liabil-ities	+ Contrib Capital	+ Earned Capital	Rev-enues	− Expen-ses	= Net Income
DE 610 AD 610 DE 610 | AD |610	a. Adjusting entry for depreciation of equipment	−610 Accum. Deprecia-tion	=			−610 Retained Earnings		+610 − Deprecia-tion Expense	= −610
SUPE 1,890 SUP 1,890 SUPE 1,890 | SUP |1,890	b. Adjusting entry for supplies expense	−1,890 Supplies	=			−1,890 Retained Earnings		+1,890 − Supplies Expense	= −1,890
UE 390 AP 390 UE 390 | AP |390	c. Adjusting entry for utilities expense		=	+390 Accounts (Utilities) Payable		−390 Retained Earnings		+390 − Utilities Expense	= −390
RNTE 700 PPRNT 700 RNTE 700 | PPRNT |700	d. Adjusting entry for rent expense	−700 Prepaid Rent	=			−700 Retained Earnings		+700 − Rent Expense	= −700
UR 468 Rev 468 UR 468 | Rev |468	e. Adjusting entry for premium revenues		=	−468 Unearned premium revenue		+468 Retained Earnings	+468 Premium Revenue	−	= +468
WE 965 WP 965 WE 965 | WP |965	f. Adjusting entry for wages expense		=	+965 Wages Payable		−965 Retained Earnings		+965 − Wages Expense	= −965

E3-26—continued

```
AR    300
 OI       300
```

```
      AR
    300|
      OI
        |300
```

g. Adjusting entry for interest earned

+300 Interest receivable	=	+300 Retained Earnings / +300 Interest (Other) Income − = +300

E3-28 (15 minutes)

a.

```
WE    4,700
 WP       4,700
      WE
  4,700|
      WP
        |4,700
```

Transaction	Balance Sheet					Income Statement		
	Cash Asset	+ Noncash Assets	= Liabil- ities	+ Contrib Capital	+ Earned Capital	Rev- enues	− Expen- ses	= Net Income
Adjusting entry for salaries owed at year end 2006			+4,700 = Wages Payable		-4,700 Retained Earnings		+4,700 − Wages Expense	= -4,700

b.

```
WE    7,300
WP    4,700
 Cash    12,000
      WE
  7,300|
      WP
  4700|
      Cash
        |12,000
```

Transaction	Balance Sheet					Income Statement		
	Cash Asset	+ Noncash Assets	= Liabil- ities	+ Contrib Capital	+ Earned Capital	Rev- enues	− Expen- ses	= Net Income
Record salaries paid in 2007	-12,000 Cash		-4,700 = Wages Payable		-7,300 Retained Earnings		+7,300 − Wages Expense	= -7,300

E3-30 (15 minutes)

a. Balance, January 1 = $960 + $800 − $620 = $1,140.

b. Amount of premium = $82 × 12 = $984.
   Therefore, five months' premium ($984 − $574 = $410) has expired by January 31. The policy term began on September 1 of the previous year.

c. Wages paid in January = $3,200 − $500 = $2,700.

d. Monthly depreciation expense = $8,700 / 60 months = $145.
   Bloomfield has owned the truck for 18 months ($2,610 / $145 = 18).

E3-32 (25 minutes)

a. July 31   Rent Expense... 475

              Prepaid Rent..   475

              To record July rent expense ($5,700 / 12 = $475).

b.   31   Advertising Expense.. 210

              Prepaid Advertising..   210

              To record July advertising expense ($630 / 3 = $210).

c.   31   Supplies Expense.. 1,900

              Supplies...   1,900

              To record supplies expense

              for July ($3,000 – $1,100 = $1,900).

d.   31   Fees (Accounts) Receivable................................... 800

              Refinishing Fees Revenue..................................   800

              To record unbilled revenue earned during July.

e.   31   Unearned Refinishing Revenue.............................. 300

              Refinishing Fees Revenue..................................   300

              To record portion of advance fees earned in July ($600/2=$300).

Prepaid Rent			
Bal.	5,700	475	(a)
Bal.	5,225		

Supplies			
Bal.	3,000	1,900	(c)
Bal.	1,100		

Unearned Refinishing Fees			
(e)	300	600	Bal.
		300	Bal.

Prepaid Advertising			
Bal.	630	210	(b)
Bal.	420		

Refinishing Fees Revenue			
		2,500	Bal.
		800	(d)
		300	(e)
		3,600	Bal.

Rent Expense		
(a)	475	

Supplies Expense		
(c)	1,900	

Advertising Expense		
(b)	210	

Fees Receivable		
(d)	800	

E3-34 (10 minutes)

Cost of Goods Sold	3,301,715*	
Inventory...		3,301,715

To recognize the cost of goods sold.

*$226,893 + $3,296,240 - $221,418 = $3,301,715

Cash..	1,004,635**	
Accounts Receivable		1,004,635

To record cash collected from customers.

**$122,087 + $1,003,881 – $121,333 = $1,004,635.

E3-36 (20 minutes)

a.

Cash 1,119,833
  UR   1,119,833

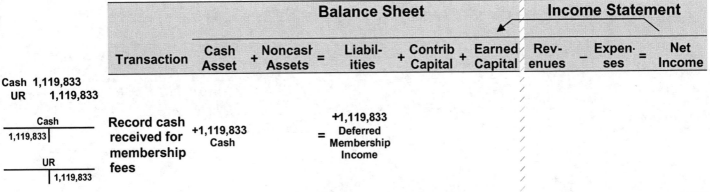

		Balance Sheet					Income Statement		
Transaction	Cash Asset	+ Noncash Assets =	Liabil- ities	+ Contrib Capital	+ Earned Capital	Rev- enues	– Expen- ses	=	Net Income
Record cash received for membership fees	+1,119,833 Cash	=	+1,119,833 Deferred Membership Income						

b. **We calculate membership fee income using the opening and closing deferred membership income balances and the cash received from members during the year, as follows: $453,881 + 1,119,833 – 500,558 = $1,073,156**

UR 1,073,156
 Rev   1,073,156

		Balance Sheet					Income Statement		
Transaction	Cash Asset	+ Noncash Assets =	Liabil- ities	+ Contrib Capital	+ Earned Capital	Revenues	– Expen- ses	=	Net Income
Recognize membership revenue		=	-1,073,156 Deferred Member- ship Income		+1,073,156 Retained Earnings	+1,073,156 Member- ship Fee Income	–	=	+1,073,156

c.

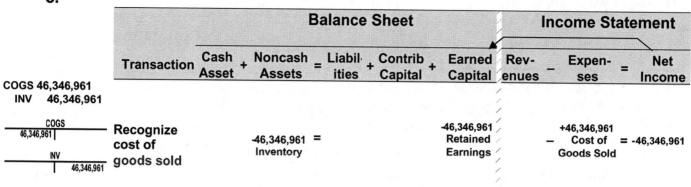

COGS 46,346,961
INV 46,346,961

Transaction	Cash Asset	+	Noncash Assets	=	Liabilities	+	Contrib Capital	+	Earned Capital	Revenues	−	Expenses	=	Net Income
Recognize cost of goods sold			-46,346,961 Inventory	=					-46,346,961 Retained Earnings		−	+46,346,961 Cost of Goods Sold	=	-46,346,961

COGS
46,346,961 |

INV
| 46,346,961

d. We calculate inventory purchases using the opening and closing balances from the inventory account and the COGS during the year, as follows: $4,014,699 + 46,346,961 - 3,643,585 = $46,718,075

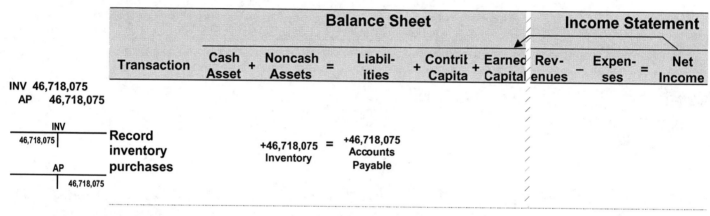

INV 46,718,075
AP 46,718,075

Transaction	Cash Asset	+	Noncash Assets	=	Liabilities	+	Contrib Capital	+	Earned Capital	Revenues	−	Expenses	=	Net Income
Record inventory purchases			+46,718,075 Inventory	=	+46,718,075 Accounts Payable						−		=	

INV
46,718,075 |

AP
| 46,718,075

E3-38^A (40 minutes)

a.

Beneish Corporation
Income Statement
For Year Ended December 31, 2008

Service fees earned	$71,000
Rent expense	(18,000)
Salaries expense	(37,100)
Depreciation expense	(7,000)
Net income	$ 8,900

Beneish Corporation Statement of Stockholders' Equity For Year Ended December 31, 2008	Common Stock	Retained Earnings	Total Stock-holders' Equity
Balance at December 31, 2007	$43,000	$20,600	$63,600
Stock issuance			
Dividends		(8,000)	(8,000)
Net income		8,900	8,900
Balance at December 31, 2008	$43,000	$21,500	$64,500

Beneish Corporation
Balance Sheet
December 31, 2008

Cash..	$ 4,000	Notes payable	$10,000
Accounts receivable	6,500	Total liabilities........................	10,000
Equipment, gross	78,000		
Accumulated depreciation	(14,000)	Common stock........................	43,000
Equipment, net	64,000	Retained earnings	21,500
Total assets............................	$74,500	Total liabilities and equity	$74,500

b.

1.	Service Fees Earned	71,000	
	Retained Earnings...		71,000
2.	Retained Earnings..	18,000	
	Rent Expense...		18,000
3.	Retained Earnings..	37,100	
	Salaries Expense...		37,100
4.	Retained Earnings..	7,000	
	Depreciation Expense.....................................		7,000
5.	Retained Earnings..	8,000	
	Dividends		8,000

c. Note: Only the ledger accounts affected by closing process are shown here.

Retained Earnings				
		20,600	Bal.	
(2)	18,000	(1)	71,000	
(3)	37,100			
(4)	7,000			
(5)	8,000			
		21,500	Bal.	

Service Fees Earned				
(1)	71,000	71,000	Bal.	
		0	Bal.	

Rent Expense			
Bal.	18,000	18,000	(2)
Bal	0		

Depreciation Expense			
Bal.	7,000	7,000	(4)
Bal	0		

Dividends			
Bal.	8,000	8,000	(5)
Bal.	0		

Salaries Expense			
Bal.	37,100	37,100	(3)
Bal.	0		

PROBLEMS

P3-40 (20 minutes)

Date		Description	Debit	Credit
Dec	31	Salaries Expense	720	
		Salaries Payable		720
		To accrue salaries at December 31		
		($1,800 × 2/5 = $720).		
	31	Interest Expense	200	
		Interest Payable		200
		To accrue interest expense at December 31.		
	31	Fees Receivable	900	
		Printing Revenue		900
		To record revenue earned but not yet billed.		
	31	Maintenance Expense	400	
		Prepaid Maintenance		400
		To record December maintenance expense.		
	31	Advertising Expense	300	
		Prepaid Advertising		300
		To record December advertising expense		
		($900 × 1/3 = $300).		
	31	Rent Expense	160	
		Rent Payable		160
		To accrue one-half month's rent expense		
		[(400 × $0.80)/2 = $160].		
	31	Interest Receivable	38	
		Interest Income		38
		To accrue interest earned in December.		
	31	Depreciation Expense—Equipment	2,175	
		Accumulated Depreciation—Equipment		2,175
		To record annual depreciation on equipment.		

P3-42 (25 minutes)

Date 2006	Description	Debit	Credit
Dec. 31	Advertising Expense	400	
	Prepaid Advertising		400
	To record advertising expense ($1,200 − $800 = $400).		
31	Wages Expense	1,300	
	Wages Payable		1,300
	To record accrued wages.		
31	Insurance Expense	1,140	
	Prepaid Insurance		1,140
	To record insurance expense ($3,420 − $2,280 = $1,140).		
31	Unearned Service Fees	2,400	
	Service Fees Earned		2,400
	To recognize fees earned ($5,400 − $3,000 = $2,400).		
31	Rent Receivable	1,000	
	Rental Income		1,000
	To record rent earned but not yet recorded.		

Date 2007	Description	Debit	Credit
Jan. 4	Wages Payable	1,300	
	Wages Expense	1,100	
	Cash		2,400
	To record payment of wages.		
4	Cash	1,000	
	Rent Receivable		1,000
	To record collection of rent.		

P3-44 (25 minutes)

a.

		Balance Sheet					Income Statement		
	Transaction	Cash Asset	+ Noncash Assets	= Liabil- ities	+ Contrib. Capital	+ Earned Capita	Rev- enues	− Expen- ses	= Net Income
Cash 11,500 CS 11,500 Cash 11,500 ∣ CS ∣ 11,500	Apr. 1. Cash received for stock	+11,500 Cash		=	+11,500 Common stock				=
PPE 6,100 Cash 6,100 PPE 6,100 ∣ Cash ∣ 6,100	Apr. 2. Purchase truck for cash	-6,100 Cash	+ 6,100 Truck	=					=
PPE 3,100 AP 2,100 Cash 1,000 PPE 3,100 ∣ AP ∣ 2,100 Cash ∣ 1.000	Apr. 2. Purchase equipment	-1,000 Cash	+3,100 Equipment	= +2,100 Accounts Payable					=
PPI 2,880 Cash 2,880 PPI 2,880 ∣ Cash ∣ 2,880	Apr. 3. Purchase liability insurance	-2,880 Cash	+2,880 Prepaid insurance	=					=
SUP 1,200 AP 1,200 SUP 1,200 ∣ AP ∣ 1,200	Apr. 5. Purchase supplies on account		+ 1,200 Supplies	= +1,200 Accounts Payable					=
Cash 1,800 UR 1,800 Cash 1,800 ∣ UR ∣ 1,800	Apr. 5. Cash in advance for roofing repairs	+1,800 Cash		= +1,800 Unearned roofing fees					=

©Cambridge Business Publishers, 2008

		Balance Sheet					Income Statement		
Transaction	Cash Asset	+ Noncash Assets	= Liabilities	+ Contrib Capital	+ Earned Capital	Revenues	− Expenses	= Net Income

AR 5,500
  Rev   5,500

AR	
5,500	

Rev	
	5,500

Apr. 12. Bill customers for services. | | +5,500 Accounts Receivable = | | | +5,500 Retained Earnings | +5,500 Roofing Fees Revenue | | = +5,500

Cash 4,900
  AR   4,900

Cash	
4,900	

AR	
	4,900

Apr. 18. Cash collected on account | +4,900 Cash | −4,900 Accounts Receivable = | | | | | | =

OE 675
  Cash   675

OE	
675	

Cash	
	675

Apr. 29. Paid cash for fuel | −675 Cash | = | | | −675 Retained Earnings | | +675 Fuel (Operating) Expense | = −675

AE 100
  Cash   100

AE	
100	

Cash	
	100

Apr. 30. Paid cash for ads | −100 Cash | = | | | −100 Retained Earnings | | +100 Advertising Expense | = −100

WE 2,500
  Cash   2,500

WE	
2,500	

Cash	
	2,500

Apr. 30. paid cash wages | −2,500 Cash | = | | | −2,500 Retained Earnings | | +2,500 Wages Expense | = −2,500

AR 4,000
  Rev   4,000

AR	
4,000	

Rev	
	4,000

Apr. 30. Bill customers for services | | +4,000 Accounts Receivable = | | | +4,000 Retained Earnings | +4,000 Roofing Fees Revenue | | = +4,000

P3-44—continued

b.

			Balance Sheet						Income Statement		
	Transaction	Cash Asset	+	Noncash Assets	=	Liabil-ities	+ Contrib Capital +	Earned Capital	Rev-enues	− Expen-ses	= Net Income
IE 120 PPI 120 INSE 120 PPI |120	1. Recognize one month of insurance expense	-120 Prepaid Insurance	=				-120 Retained Earnings		+120 − Insurance Expense	= -120
SUPE 800 SUP 800 SUPE 800| SUP |800	2. Recognize supplies expense	-800 Supplies	=				-800 Retained Earnings		+800 − Supplies Expense	= -800
DE 125 AD 125 DE 125| AD |125	3. Recognize depreciation expense - Trucks	-125 Accum. Depr'n --Trucks*	=				-125 Retained Earnings		+125 − Depreciation Expense	= -125
DE 35 AD 35 DE 35| AD |35	4. Recognize depreciation expense - Equipment	-35 Accum. Depr'n –Equipment*	=				-35 Retained Earnings		+35 − Depreciation Expense	= -35
UR 450 Rev 450 UR 450| Rev |450	5. Recognize roofing fees earned		=	-450 Unearned Roofing Fees			+450 Retained Earnings	+450 Roofing Fees Revenue	−	= +450

P3-46 (30 minutes)

a.

Date 2008	Description	Debit	Credit
Dec. 31	Fees Receivable..	925	
	Photography Fees Earned		925
	To record revenue earned but not billed.		
31	Depreciation Expense......................................	2,280	
	Accumulated Depreciation—Equipment		2,280
	To record depreciation for the year		
	($22,800 / 10 years = $2,280).		
31	Utilities Expense..	400	
	Utilities Payable		400
	To record estimated December utilities expense.		
31	Rent Expense...	6,300	
	Prepaid Rent..		6,300
	To record rent expense for the year		
	($12,600 / 2 years = $6,300).		
31	Unearned Photography Fees.............................	2,600	
	Photography Fees Earned		2,600
	To record advance payments earned.		
31	Insurance Expense..	990	
	Prepaid Insurance..		990
	To record insurance expense for		
	the year ($2,970 / 3 years = $990).		
31	Supplies Expense..	2,730	
	Supplies..		2,730
	To record supplies expense for the year		
	($4,250 – $1,520 = $2,730).		
31	Wages Expense..	375	
	Wages Payable..		375
	To record unpaid wages at December 31.		

P3-46—continued.

b.

Cash			
Unadj. bal	2,150		
Adj. Bal.	2,150		

Accounts Receivable			
Unadj. bal	3,800		
Adj. Bal.	3,800		

Fees Receivable			
Dec. 31	(1) 925		
Adj. Bal.	925		

Prepaid Rent			
Unadj. bal	12,600	6,300 (4)	Dec.31
Adj. Bal.	6,300		

Prepaid Insurance			
Unadj. bal	2,970	990 (6)	Dec.31
Adj. Bal.	1,980		

Supplies			
Unadj. bal	4,250	2,730 (7)	Dec.31
Adj. Bal.	1,520		

Equipment			
Unadj. bal	22,800		
Adj. Bal.	22,800		

Accum. Depreciation - Equip			
		2,280 (2)	Dec.31
		2,280	Adj. Bal.

Supplies Expense			
Dec. 31	(7) 2,730		
Adj. Bal.	2,730		

Insurance Expense			
Dec. 31	(6) 990		
Adj. Bal.	990		

Accounts Payable			
		1,910	Unadj. bal
		1,910	Adj. Bal.

Unearned Photo Fees			
Dec. 31	(5) 2,600	2,600	Unadj. bal
		0	Adj. Bal.

Utilities Payable			
		400 (3)	Dec.31
		400	Adj. Bal.

Wages Payable			
		375 (8)	Dec.31
		375	Adj. Bal.

Common Stock			
		24,000	Unadj. bal
		24,000	Adj. Bal.

Photo Fees Earned			
		34,480	Unadj. bal
		925 (1)	Dec.31
		2,600 (5)	Dec.31
		38,005	Adj. Bal.

Wages Expense			
Unadj. bal	11,000		
Dec.31	(8) 375		
Adj. Bal.	11,375		

Utilities Expense			
Unadj. bal	3,420		
Dec.31	(3) 400		
Adj. Bal.	3,820		

Depreciation Expense - Equip			
Dec.31	(2) 2,280		
Adj. Bal.	2,280		

Rent Expense			
Dec.31	(4) 6,300		
Adj. Bal.	6,300		

P3-48 (35 minutes)

a.

Date 2008	Description	Debit	Credit
Dec. 31	Advertising Expense	1,540	
	Prepaid Advertising		1,540
	To record 11 months' advertising expense ($1,680 × 11/12 = $1,540).		
31	Depreciation Expense	5,280	
	Accumulated Depreciation		5,280
	To record depreciation for the year ($42,240 / 8 years = $5,280).		
31	Utilities Expense	325	
	Accounts Payable		325
	To record estimated December utilities expense.		
31	Wages Expense	1,200	
	Wages Payable		1,200
	To record unpaid wages at December 31.		
31	Supplies Expense	4,750	
	Supplies		4,750
	To record supplies expense for the year ($6,270 – $1,520 = $4,750).		
31	Interest Expense	450	
	Interest Payable		450
	To accrue interest expense at December 31.		
31	Rent Expense	430	
	Accounts Payable		430
	To record additional rent owed under lease (1/2% × $86,000 = $430).		

P3-48—continued.

b.
Note: only required T-accounts are shown here.

Accounts Payable		
	2,700	Bal.
	325	3.
	430	7.

Prepaid Advertising			
Bal.	1,680	1,540	1.

Supplies			
Bal.	6,270	4,750	5.

Accumulated Depreciation Equipment		
	5,280	2

Advertising Expense		
1.	1,540	

Interest Payable		
	450	6

Rent Expense		
Bal.	6,300	
7.	430	

Wages Expense		
Bal.	38,800	
4.	1,200	

Depreciation Expense		
2.	5,280	

Utilities Expense		
Bal.	3,020	
3.	325	

Wages Payable		
	1,200	4.

Supplies Expense		
5.	4,750	

Interest Expense		
6.	450	

CASES

C3-50 (60 minutes)

a.

The financial statement effects template first shows the initial deposits and checks. These are entries 1- 8. Entries a - f are the adjusting entries that would be made at the end of the three months. Expenditures for rent and salaries are assumed to have been initially debited to expense accounts.

	Transaction	Balance Sheet					Income Statement		
		Cash Asset	+ Noncash Assets	= Liabil-ities	+ Contrib. Capital	+ Earned Capital	Rev-enues	− Expen-ses	= Net Income
Cash 50,000 CS 50,000 Cash 50,000 | CS |50,000	1. Cash investment	+50,000 Cash		=	+50,000 Common Stock				=
Cash 81,000 Rev 81,000 Cash 81,000 | Rev |81,000	2. Collections from customers	+81,000 Cash		=		+81,000 Retained Earnings	+81,000 Sales revenues		= +81,000
Cash 10,000 NP 10,000 Cash 10,000 | NP |10,000	3. Bank borrowing	+10,000 Cash		= +10,000 Notes payable					=
RNTE 24,000 Cash 24,000 RNTE 24,000 | Cash |24,000	4. Rent expense	-24,000 Cash		=		-24,000 Retained Earnings		+24,000 Rent expanse	= -24,000
PPE 25,000 Cash 25,000 PPE 25,000 | Cash |25,000	5. Purchased equipment	-25,000 Cash	+25,000 Equipment	=					=

C3-50—continued

	Transaction	Cash Asset	+	Noncash Assets	=	Liabil-ities	+	Contrib Capital	+	Earned Capital	Rev-enues	−	Expen-ses	=	Net Income
INV 62,000 Cash 62,000 INV 62,000 Cash 62,000	6. Purchased inventory	-62,000 Cash		+62,000 Inventory	=										=	
WE 6,000 Cash 6,000 WE 6,000 Cash 6,000	7. Paid salaries	-6,000 Cash			=						-6,000 Retained Earnings		−	+6,000 Salaries Expense	=	-6,000
OE 13,000 Cash 13,000 OE 13,000 Cash 13,000	8. Paid other expenses	-13,000 Cash			=						-13,000 Retained Earnings		−	+13,000 Misc. (Operating) Expenses	=	-13,000
AR 9,000 Rev 9,000 AR 9,000 Rev 9,000	a. Recognize credit sales			+9,000 A/R	=						+9,000 Retained Earnings	+9,000 Sales Revenue			=	+9,000
PPRNT 12,000 RNTE 12,000 PPRNT 12,000 RNTE 12,000	b. Adjust rent expense			+12,000 Prepaid Rent	=						+12,000 Retained Earnings		−	-12,000 Rent Expense	=	+12,000
WE 3,000 WP 3,000 WE 3,000 WP 3,000	c. Accrue salaries expense				=	+3,000 Salaries payable					-3,000 Retained Earnings		−	+3,000 Salaries Expense	=	-3,000

C3-50—continued

		Balance Sheet				Income Statement		
Transaction	Cash Asset	+ Noncash Assets	= Liabil- ities	+ Contrib Capital	+ Earned Capital	Rev- enues	– Expen- ses	= Net Income
d. Recognize cost of goods sold		−41,000 Inventory =			−41,000 Retained Earnings		+41,000 Cost of Goods Sold	= −41,000
e. Accrue depreciation expense		− 1,250 Accum. = Depr'n			−1,250 Retained Earnings		+1,250 – Depreciation = Expense	−1,250
f. Accrue interest expense*		=	+300 Interest Payable (Accrued)		−300 Retained Earnings		+300 – Interest = Expense	−300

COGS 1,200
INV 1,200

COGS 41,000 |
INV | 41,000

DE 1,250
AD 1,250

DE 1,250 |
AD | 1,250

IE 300
ACC 300

IE 300 |
ACC | 300

Journal entries are shown in the financial statements effects template for all entries and below again for the adjustments a-f.

a. Accounts Receivable 9,000
　　　　Sales Revenue .... 　　9,000
　　　To recognize sales on account.

b. Prepaid Rent 12,000
　　　　Rent Expense... 　12,000
　　　To recognize remaining prepaid rent and
　　　correct rent expense to ½ of $24,000.

c. Salary Expense.. 3,000
　　　　Salaries Payable .... 　　3,000
　　　To recognize prepaid salaries for September.

d. Cost of Goods Sold.. 41,000
　　　　Merchandise Inventory .... 　41,000
　　　To recognize cost of sales. ($62,000 - $21,000)

C3-50—continued

e. Depreciation Expense... 1,250

     Accumulated Depreciation 1,250

     To accrue depreciation on the fixtures
     and equipment. ($25,000 / 5 years × 3 months /12)

f. Interest Expense... 300

     Interest Accrued Payable 300

     To accrue interest on bank loan.
     ($10,000) × 0.12 × 3/12

The balances shown are the amounts in the accounts prior to the entry of the adjustments described in items a through f. The cash balance represents the deposits made $141,000 less the checks drawn $130,000.

Cash				Inventory			
Bal.	11,000			Bal.	62,000	41,000	d.

			Prepaid Rent		
		b.	12,000		

Equipment		
Bal.	25,000	

Accumulated Depreciation-Equipment				Salaries Payable			
		1,250	e.			3,000	c.

Accounts Receivable				Stockholders' Equity			
a.	9,000					50,000	Bal.

Sales Revenue				Cost of Goods Sold			
		81,000	Bal.	d.	41,000		
		9,000	a.				

Rent Expense				Depreciation Expense			
Bal.	24,000	12,000	b.	e.	1,250		

C3-50—continued

Other Expense		
Bal.	13,000	

Bank Loan Payable		
	10,000	Bal.

Salaries Expense		
Bal.	6,000	
c.	3,000	

Interest Expense		
f.	300	

Interest Payable		
	300	f.

b.

Stocken Surf Shop Income Statement For Three Months Ended September 30, 2008		
Sales Revenues		$90,000
Cost of Goods Sold		41,000
Gross Margin		49,000
Expenses		
Rent Expense	$12,000	
Salaries Expense	9,000	
Depreciation Expense	1,250	
Interest Expense	300	
Other Expenses	13,000	35,550
Net Income		$13,450

Stocken Surf Shop
Balance Sheet
September 30, 2008

Assets
Current assets

Cash	$11,000
Accounts receivable	9,000
Inventory	21,000
Prepaid rent	12,000
Total current assets	53,000
Fixtures and equipment, net	23,750
Total assets	$76,750

Liabilities and equity
Current liabilities

Salaries payable	$ 3,000
Bank loan payable	10,000
Interest payable	300
Total current liabilities	13,300
Stockholders' equity ($50,000 + $13,450)*	63,450
Total liabilities and equity	$76,750

* Stockholders' equity can be separated into two accounts: Common Stock and Retained Earnings.

C3-50—continued

c.

Module 1 introduced the return on net operating assets ratio as a simple performance measure that can be used to evaluate how well this new business is doing. The return on net operating assets is calculated as the ratio of net operating profit after tax (net income before interest expense) to net operating assets (assets less financing liabilities such as loans). Because we don't have tax information in this case, we will use a pretax calculation. In this case, the return on net operating assets for the three month period was 20.6% ($13,450 + $300 interest) / ($76,750 − $10,000) loan. This is a very good return for a three month period. However, the favorable performance evaluation should be tempered by a few caveats:

(1) Retail businesses are notoriously seasonal. That is, sales (and profits) fluctuate from season to season. A business such as this one would likely have its highest sales in the second and third quarters. This seasonality must be considered when we try to annualize quarterly results like these. Once the business has operated for a year or two, the owner would likely have a better idea about how seasonal fluctuations affect sales and returns and would be better able to interpret quarterly performance measures.

(2) Stocken's cash position is precarious. The firm has burned through most of the $60,000 cash raised to begin the business ($50,000 from the owner and the $10,000 loan) and is likely to have trouble replacing its inventory as well as paying its bills. Perhaps they can convince lenders to come to their rescue. If not, the firm will not last another three months.

C3-52 (15 minutes)

a., b.

Beatty must consider the following ethical considerations:

1. Balancing the long-run interests of the firm (securing the international contract) against the short-run requirements to present accurately the financial data of the company for the current year (recording $150,000 adjusting entry).
2. Compromising the confidentiality of the contract negotiations (by disclosing the contract negotiations to additional persons) versus compromising her professional responsibilities (by omitting a significant year-end adjusting entry).
3. Jeopardizing her position with the firm (by revealing information the president wants kept secret) versus risking possible future legal action by parties relying on the firm's financial statements (by not revealing a significant accrued expense and accrued liability in the financial statements).

Beatty should consider that outside auditors frequently access confidential data and disclosing the contract negotiations to the auditor should not represent a significant breach of confidentiality. Perhaps Beatty can achieve a reasonable solution to her dilemma by suggesting that an adjusting entry be recorded and described in very general terms (for example, labeling the liability Payable to Consultants and indicating it is for marketing research and development). Such an adjustment would permit the disclosure of the significant liability without revealing important details to anyone else within or outside the company.

C3-54 (20 minutes)

a. Prepaid and deferred marketing costs 84,833

        Cash 84,833

    To record the direct costs paid for catalogs.

b. Catalog Expense 81,400

        Prepaid and deferred marketing costs 81,400

    To recognize catalog expense: ($6,905 + $84,933 - $10,438)

c. Cash 31,470

        Unearned Gift Certificate Revenues 31,470

    To recognize gift certificates sold but not redeemed.

d. Unearned Gift Certificate Revenues 27,080

        Gift Certificate Revenues 27,080

    To recognize revenues based on redeemed gift certificates:
    ($9,329 + $31,470 - $13,719)

Module 4

Analyzing and Interpreting Financial Statements

QUESTIONS

Q4-2.[B] ROE is the sum of an operating return (RNOA) and a nonoperating return (the effective use of financial leverage – specifically, leverage multiplied by the spread). Increasing leverage increases ROE as long as the spread is positive. Financial leverage is also related to risk: the risk of potential bankruptcy and the risk of increased variability of profits. Companies must, therefore, balance the positive effects of financial leverage against their potential negative consequences. It is for this reason that we do not witness companies entirely financed with debt.

Q4-4. Reducing advertising or R&D expenditures can increase current operating profit at the expense of the long-term competitive position of the firm. Expenditures on advertising or R&D are more asset-like and create long-term economic benefits.

Q4-6. ROE>RNOA implies a positive return on nonoperating activities. This results from borrowed funds being invested in operating assets whose return (RNOA) exceeds the cost of borrowing. In this case, borrowing money increases ROE.

Q4-8. The interest tax shield arises because interest expense is deductible for tax purposes. Thus, interest expense "shields" income from taxes by reducing taxable income. The after-tax cost of interest is, therefore, the pre-tax cost multiplied by 1 minus the appropriate tax rate (typically the sum of the federal and state tax rates).

Q4-10. Companies must manage both the income statement and the balance sheet in order to maximize RNOA. This is important, as many managers look only to the income statement and do not fully appreciate the value added by effective balance sheet management. The disaggregation of RNOA into its profit and turnover components facilitates analysis of these two areas of focus.

Q4-12. Liquidity refers to cash: how much cash a company has, how much cash is coming in the door, and how much cash can be raised quickly. Companies must generate cash in order to pay their debts, pay their employees and provide their shareholders a return on investment. Cash is, therefore, critical to a company's survival.

Q4-14.[A] Common size financial statements express balance sheet and income statement items in ratio form. Common-size balance sheets express each asset, liability and equity item as a percentage of total assets and common-size income statements express each line item as a percentage of sales. The ratio form facilitates comparison among firms of different sizes as well as across time for the same firm.

M4-16 (15 minutes)

($ millions)

a. Target's net operating profit *before* tax = $52,620 - $34,927 - $11,185 - $776 - $1,409 = $4,323.

Note: We treat net credit card revenues, and the related credit card expense, as operating because Target maintains its own proprietary credit card to support in-store sales. The accounts receivable relating to these credit cards is also included as an operating current asset in M4-15.

b. NOPAT = $4,323 – ($1,452 + [$463 x 0.383]) = $2,694.

Alternatively, using the 38.3% statutory tax rate yields a tax rate on net operating profit = ($1,452 + [$463 x 0.383]) / $4,323 = 37.7%.

NOPAT = $4,323 × (1- 0.377) = $2,693 ($1 rounding difference)

M4-18 (15 minutes)

($ millions)

NOA = $20,513 - $272 - $1,256 - $469 - $989 - $1,452 - $3,866 = $12,209

M4-20 (20 minutes)

($ millions)

a. RNOA   = NOPAT / Average net operating assets
         = $3,306 / [($12,209 + $12,972)/2]
         = 26.26%

b. NOPM   = NOPAT / Sales = $3,306 / $21,167 = 15.62%

   NOAT   = Sales / Average NOA = $21,167 / [($12,209 + $12,972)/2]
          = 1.68

   RNOA   = NOPM x NOAT = 15.62% x 1.68 = 26.24% (.02% rounding error)

M4-22 (15 minutes)

($ millions)

a. Verizon's current ratio for the two years presented is as follows:

2005 current ratio: $16,448 / $25,063 = 0.66

2004 current ratio: $19,479 / 23,129 = 0.84

Liquidity is decreasing and this is not a good trend. Moreover, current ratio is significantly below 1.0. We might want to know, however, whether Verizon's current assets are concentrated in cash or relatively illiquid inventories, as well as the maturity schedule of its current liabilities. We would also like to know the average current ratio for the industry. This would help place Verizon's numbers in perspective.

b. Verizon's times interest earned ratio for the two years is as follows:

2005 times interest earned = $12,787 / $2,180 = 5.87
2004 times interest earned = $12,496 / 2,384 = 5.24

Verizon's times interest earned ratio has increased, but its level is not high.

2005 total liabilities-to-equity = $101,696 / $66,434 = 1.53
2004 total liabilities-to-equity = $103,345 / $62,613 = 1.65

Verizon's total liabilities-to-equity ratio has declined, but is in excess of the 1.13 median for companies in the telecommunications industry.

Verizon's net operating cash flow to total liabilities ratios are as follows:
2005 net operating cash flow to total liabilities= $22,012 / $101,696 = 0.22
2004 net operating cash flow to total liabilities= $21,820 / $103,345 = 0.21

Verizon's net operating cash flow to total liabilities ratio has increased slightly, which is good news.

c. Verizon is carrying a significant amount of debt. Although its profitability and operating cash flow are fairly strong, neither are particularly high in relation to the company's liabilities and interest costs. There is some question, therefore, regarding the amount of additional debt that the company can take on. Given its significant capital expenditure requirements and its current debt load, Verizon may have to fund future capital expenditures with higher cost equity. And, to the extent that its competitors are not as highly leveraged, this may negatively impact Verizon's competitive position.

©Cambridge Business Publishers, 2008

EXERCISES

E4-24 (30 minutes)

a.

($ millions)	RNOA
Target Corp	$2,693 / [($24,077 + $22,567)/2] = 11.55%
Wal-Mart Stores	$12,290 / [($93,457+$81,788)/2] = 14.03%

b.

($ millions)	NOPM = NOPAT / Sales	NOAT = Sales / Average NOA
Target Corp	$2,693/$52,620 = 5.12%	$52,620/[($24,077+$22,567)/2] = 2.26
Wal-Mart Stores	$12,290/$312,427= 3.93%	$312,427/[($93,457+$81,788)/2]=3.57

c. Wal-Mart's RNOA is greater than Target's in fiscal 2006. Wal-Mart's value pricing strategy is clearly evident in its lower NOPM margin, but this is more than offset by a higher turnover of net operating assets and, hence, Wal-Mart's business model is somewhat more successful.

E4-26 (30 minutes)

a.

($ millions)	RNOA
CVS Corp	$1,292 / [($10,520+$9,829) / 2] = 12.70%
Walgreen Co	$1,539 / [($8,395+$6,888) / 2] = 20.14%

b.

($ millions)	NOPM = NOPAT / Sales	NOAT = Sales / Average NOA
CVS Corp	$1,292/$37,006=3.49%	$37,006/[($10,520+$9,829)/2]=3.64
Walgreen Co ...	$1,539/$42,202=3.65%	$42,202/[($8,395+$6,888)/2]= 5.52

c. Walgreen's RNOA is higher than CVS'. The low NOPMs for both companies reflect the highly competitive retail pharmaceutical industry. Walgreen's advantage lies in its net operating asset turnover rate which is 52% greater than CVS'. Walgreen is more efficient with its assets, which makes the company more profitable overall.

E4-28 (30 minutes)

a.

($ millions)	
ROE	$834 / [($4,425+$4,115)/2] = 19.53%
RNOA	$832 / [($4,367+$4,202)/2] = 19.42%

b.

($ millions)	NOPM = NOPAT / Sales	NOAT = Sales / Average NOA
Staples	$832/$16,079=5.17%	$16,079/[($4,367+$4,202)/2]=3.75

c. RNOA/ROE=99%. Staples' debt is financing assets that earn a return just slightly in excess of the cost of debt, thus slightly improving the returns to shareholders. This could mean that the company is holding a high level of marketable securities relative to debt.

Staples' NOPM is relatively low indicating that the company is in a highly competitive industry. This is due to Staples product (office supplies) being an undifferentiated product. On the other hand, NOAT is relatively high (say compared to companies in the manufacturing or telecom industry) because Staples is not capital intensive and turns inventory over frequently. The two components together, cause Staples to have a high RNOA, higher than the average U.S. industrial.

E4-30 (30 minutes)

a.

($ millions)	Current Ratio
2003	$5,403 / $9,654 = 0.56
2004	$3,535 / $8,635 = 0.41
2005	$2,594 / $6,269 = 0.41

Comcast has a current ratio less than 1.0 and it has declined from 2003 levels. Comcast is not very liquid. While the current ratio provides a useful point estimate of liquidity, it would be helpful to know when the cash flows from current assets will be realized and when the current liabilities will need to be paid. An excess of current maturities over near-term cash realization will cause a liquidity problem regardless of the level of the overall ratio. As well, we would like to know the current ratio for firms in this industry.

b.

($ millions)	Times interest earned	Total liabilities / stockholders' equity
2003	$[(137)+2,018] / $2,018 = 0.93	$67,105 / $42,054 = 1.60
2004	$(1,810+1,807) / $1,807 = 2.00	$62,804 / $41,890 = 1.50
2005	$(1,880 + 1,796) / $1,796 = 2.05	$62,270 / $40,876 = 1.52

The times interest earned ratio has steadily climbed since 2003. It is low in 2003 because Comcast had a net loss that year. However, the ratio is low and Comcast is able to cover its interest expense, but not with a comfortable margin. Comcast's total liabilities-to-stockholders' equity ratio is relatively high between 1.50 and 1.60, and has remained fairly constant over the three-year period.

c. Comcast has a relatively high level of debt. This, coupled with its relatively low liquidity, and low earnings and cash flow relative to its interest charges and debt levels, respectively, cause some concern about its ability to increase its debt load significantly. This is especially troublesome given the significant levels of capital expenditures that will be required in order to upgrade its infrastructure in order to remain competitive with Verizon.

E4-32 (30 minutes)

a.

($ millions)	Times interest earned	Total liabilities / stockholders' equity
Industrial............	($21,025+ $1,432)/$1,432 = 15.68	$74,599 / $109,354 = 0.68
Financial	($10,246+$14,308)/$14,308 = 1.72	$487,542 / $50,815 = 9.59
Total	($22,129+$15,187)/$15,187 = 2.46	$555,934 / $109,354 = 5.08

a. GE's overall times interest earned of 2.46 is not particularly high, and its total liabilities-to-stockholders' equity is relatively high. Most of the debt, however, is concentrated in the financial services segment. This segment has the profile of a typical financial institution, with high debt levels and relatively low operating margins. As long as GE's loans and leases are of good quality (are collectible), the financial subsidiary should have no problem meeting its debt requirements as the cash flows received from its loans/leases are typically well matched with the debt payment requirements.

b. Consolidated financial statements combine the performance and financial position of the parent company and all of its subsidiaries. As such, they are a blend of financial statements from a variety of companies. Segment analysis is often useful in order to evaluate the financial structure of each segment against its respective business model. In this case, the relatively high debt level for GE as a whole is a blend of the less-financially leveraged manufacturing subsidiary with the highly leveraged financial services subsidiary.

©Cambridge Business Publishers, 2008

E4-34 (20 minutes)

The following table shows the calculations for taxes on operating and nonoperating items.

TJX 2006	Net Operating Profit	Nonoperating Expense	Total Profit
Before Tax	$1,038,959	$29,632	$1,009,327
Tax	330,181	11,260	318,904
After Tax	708,778	18,372	690,423

TJX 2005	Net Operating Profit	Nonoperating Expense	Total Profit
Before Tax	$1,014,708	$25,757	$988,951
Tax	389,039	9,788	379,252
After Tax	625,669	15,969	609,699

a.

2006 Tax Shield = $11,260 (computed as $29,632 x 0.38)
2005 Tax Shield = $9,788   (computed as $25,757 x 0.38)

b.

2006 Tax Rate on Net Operating Profit = 31.78%,
  computed as ($318,904 + $11,260) / $1,038,959

2005 Tax Rate on Net Operating Profit = 38.34%,
  computed as ($379,252 + $9,788) / $1,014,708

c.

2006 NOPAT = $1,038,959 x (1- 0.3178) = $708,778
2005 NOPAT = $1,014,708 x (1- 0.3834) = $625,669

PROBLEMS

P4-36 (30 minutes)

a.

2005 current ratio = $10,529 / $9,428 = 1.12
2004 current ratio = $8,953 / $8,566 = 1.05

2005 quick ratio = ($2,244 + $429 + $4,579) / $9,428 = 0.77
2004 quick ratio = ($1,060 + $396 + $4,094) / $8,566 = 0.65

Both the current and quick ratios have increased during 2005, but neither are high. Lockheed Martin is not particularly liquid.

b.

2005 times interest earned = ($2,616 + $370) / $370 = 8.07
2004 times interest earned = ($1,664 + $425) / $425 = 4.92

2005 total liabilities-to-stockholders' equity = ($9,428 + $4,784 + $2,097 + $1,277 + $2,291) / $7,867 = 2.53
2004 total liabilities-to-stockholders' equity = ($8,566 + $5,104 + $1,660 + $1,236 + $1,967) / $7,021 = 2.64

Lockheed Martin's times interest earned increased significantly during 2005, due to both an increase in profitability and a decrease in interest expense. Its total liabilities-to-stockholders' equity also decreased, but remains at a relatively high level.

c. Lockheed Martin is not particularly liquid and is financially leveraged. Its times interest earned ratio is high, thus lessening any solvency concerns. The company's ability to meet its debt requirements will depend on its continued profitability.

P4-38 (45 minutes)

($millions)

a.
2006 NOPAT = $4,323 – ($1,452 + [$463 x 0.383]) = $2,694
2005 NOPAT = $3,601 – ($1,146 + [$570 x 0.383]) = $2,237

b.
2006 NOA = ($34,995) – ($6,268 + $2,193 + $374 + $851 + $1,232) = $24,077
2005 NOA = ($32,293) – ($5,779 + $1,633 + $304 + $973 + $1,037) = $22,567

c.
2006 RNOA = $2,694 / [($24,077 + $22,567) / 2] = 11.55%
2005 RNOA = $2,237 / [($22,567 + $21,307) / 2] = 10.20%

2006 NOPM = $2,694 / $52,620 = 5.12%
2005 NOPM = $2,237 / $46,839 = 4.78%

2006 NOAT = $52,620 / [($24,077 + $22,567) / 2] = 2.26
2005 NOAT = $46,839 / [($22,567 + $21,307) / 2] = 2.14

Target's RNOA increased from 2005 to 2006. Both the NOPM and the NOAT increased, with the increase in NOPM being the primary driver of the overall RNOA increase.

d.
2006 NNO = $753 + $9,119 = $9,872
Confirm:
2006 NOA =   NNO +   SE
  $24,077   = $9,872 + $14,205

2005 NNO = $504 + $9,034 = $9,538
Confirm:
2005 NOA =   NNO +   SE
  $22,567   = $9,538 + $13,029

P4-38—continued

e.

2006 ROE = $2,408 / ([$14,205 + $13,029] / 2) = 17.68%
2005 ROE = $3,198 / ([$13,029 + $11,132] / 2) = 26.47%

f.

2006 nonoperating return = ROE – RNOA = 17.68% – 11.55% = 6.13%
2005 nonoperating return = ROE – RNOA = 26.47% – 10.20% = 16.27%

g. ROE > RNOA implies that Target is able to borrow money to fund operating assets that yield a return greater than the cost of the debt. The excess accrues to the benefit of Target's stockholders. The net nonoperating expense percent in 2005 is impacted significantly by earnings on discontinued operations and gains on their sale which are customarily categorized as nonoperating.

P4-40[B] (40 minutes)

a.

2006 NNO = [$753 + $9,119] = $9,872
2005 NNO = [$504 + $9,034] = $9,538

2006 FLEV = [($9,872 + $9,538) / 2] / [($14,205 + $13,029) / 2] = 0.71

NNE = NOPAT – net income = $2,694 – $2,408 = $286

NNEP = $286 / [($9,872 + $9,538) / 2] = 2.95%
Spread = RNOA – NNEP = 11.55% – 2.95% = 8.60%

b. ROE = 11.55% + (0.71 x 8.60%) = 17.66% (-0.02% rounding error)

c. Target is able to borrow funds and invest the proceeds in operating assets yielding a return in excess of the cost of the debt. The excess accrues to the benefit of its stockholders.

P4-42 (45 minutes)

(Note to instructor: This problem requires computation of ROE in the presence of minority interest. In addition, Merck's ROE<RNOA. This is an example of equity supporting the strategic investment in liquidity at some cost to ROE.)

($millions)

a.

2005 NOPAT = ($7,363.9 – $110.2) – [$2,732.6 – ($232* x 0.375)] = $4,608.1
2004 NOPAT = ($7,974.5 – $344.0) – [$2,161.1 – ($498.2* x 0.363)] = $5,650.2

	2005	2004
* Other income on the income statement........	110.2	344.0
Minority interest expense..............................	121.8	154.2
Net nonoperating income..............................	232.0	498.2

b.

2005 NOA = $44,845.8 – $6,052.3 – $1,107.9 – $471.1 – $5,381.2 – $3,649.2 – $830.0 – $6,092.9 = $21,261.2

2004 NOA = $42,572.8 – $4,211.1 – $6,727.1 – $421.4 – $5,288.1 – $3,012.3 – $841.1 – $6,442.1 = $15,629.6

c.

2005 RNOA = $4,608.1 / [($21,261.2 + $15,629.6) / 2] = 24.98%
2004 RNOA = $5,650.2 / [($15,629.6 + $15,374.4) / 2] = 36.45%

2005 NOPM = $4,608.1 / $22,011.9 = 20.93%
2004 NOPM = $5,650.26 / $22,938.6 = 24.63%

2005 NOAT = $22,011.9 / ([$21,261.2 + $15,629.6] / 2) = 1.19
2004 NOAT = $22,938.6 / ([$15,629.6 + $15,374.4] / 2) = 1.48

Merck's RNOA declined in 2005 because both NOPM and NOAT were lower than the previous year.

d.

2005 NNO = $2,972.0 + $5,125.6 – $6,052.3 – $1,107.9 = $937.4
    Confirm: $21,261.2 = $937.4 + $17,916.6 + 2,407.2

2004 NNO = $2,181.2 + $4,691.5 – $4,211.1 – $6,727.1 = $(4,065.5)
    Confirm: $15,629.6 = $(4,065.5) + $17,288.2 + 2,406.9

P4-42—continued

e.

2005 ROCE = $4,631.3 / [($17,916.6 + $17,288.2) / 2] = 26.31%
2004 ROCE = $5,813.4 / [($17,288.2 + $15,576.4) / 2] = 35.38%

2005 ROCE = ROCE before MI x MI sharing ratio

$$= \frac{4,631.3 + \$121.8\ *}{[\$17,916.6 + \$2,407.2 + \$17,288.2 + \$2,406.9] / 2} \times \left[\frac{\dfrac{\$4,631.3}{\$4,631.3 + \$121.8}}{\dfrac{\$17,916.6 + \$17,288.2}{[\$17,916.6 + \$2,407.2] + [\$17,288.2 + \$2,406.9]}} \right]$$

= 23.75% x 1.1 = 26.1%

* 2005 Minority interest expense = $121.8

f.

2005 = $3,848.0 / $22,011.9 = 17.48%
2004 = $4,010.2 / $22,938.6 = 17.48%
2003 = $3,279.9 / $22,485.9 = 14.59%

2005 sales growth = ($22,011.9 / $22,938.6) -1 = -4.04%
2004 sales growth = ($22,938.6 / $22,485.9) -1 = 2.01%
2003 sales growth = ($22,485.9 / $21,445.8) -1 = 4.85%

Merck's R&D spending increased as a percentage of sales from 2003 to 2005, yet its sales growth has declined and is negative for 2005. The effectiveness of its R&D in bringing products to market is, thus, called into question, especially given the relatively high percentage of spending on R&D (nearly 17.5%). Recall that in 2004 and 2005 Merck faced serious legal challenges to a main drug, and this could have negatively impacted sales.

P4-44 (20 minutes)

a.

2005 current ratio = $11,003 / $6,793 = 1.62
2004 current ratio = $12,605 / $6,529 = 1.93

2005 quick ratio = ($1,369 + $1,672 + $5,950 + $411) / $6,793 = 1.38
2004 quick ratio = ($739 + $4,458 + $5,156 + $524) / $6,529 = 1.67

UPS' current and quick ratios have declined from 2004 to 2005, but remain at comfortable levels.

b.

2005 times interest earned = ($6,075 + $68) / $68 = 90.34
2004 times interest earned = ($4,922 + $67) / $67 = 74.46

2005 total liabilities-to-equity = ($6,793 + $3,159 + $1,704 + $6,682) / $16,884 = 1.09
2004 total liabilities-to-equity = ($6,529 + $3,261 + $1,470 + $5,450) / $16,378 = 1.02

The times interest earned ratio has increased significantly from 2004 to 2005, while the total liabilities-to-equity ratio increased slightly and is not at a particularly high level.

c. UPS is very liquid, with a high concentration of current assets in liquid assets. Although the total liabilities-to-equity ratio has increased slightly from 2004, it remains at a fairly low level. UPS is well-capitalized and, given its high times interest earned ratio, we have no concerns about its solvency.

P4-46 (30 minutes)

a.

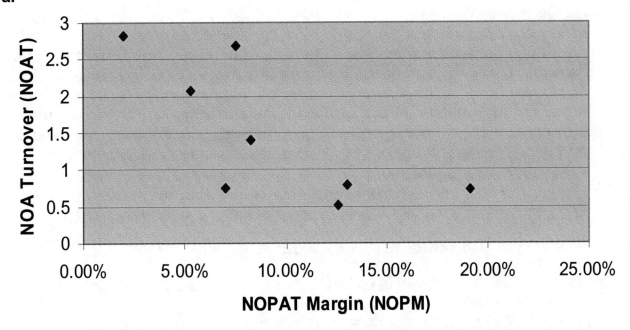

The graph reveals the margin/turnover trade-off. Firms with high turnover have low margin and vice versa.

b. High performing companies are those that exhibit a higher profit margin holding asset turnover constant, <u>and</u> have a higher turnover holding profit margin constant. Increasing RNOA requires managers to manage both the income statement <u>and</u> the balance sheet.

CASES

C4-48 (30 minutes)

a. Working capital management is an important component of the management of a company. By reducing the level of working capital, companies reduce the costs of carrying excess assets. This can have a significantly positive effect on financial performance. Some common approaches to reducing working capital via reductions in receivables and inventories, and increases in payables, include the following:
- Reduce receivables
  - Constricting the payment terms on product sales
  - Better credit policies that limit credit to high risk customers
  - Better reporting to identify delinquencies
  - Automated notices to delinquent accounts
  - Increased collection efforts
  - Pre-payment of orders or billing as milestones are reached
  - Use of electronic (ACH) payment
  - Use of third party guarantors, including bank letters of credit
- Reduce inventories
  - Reduce inventory costs via less costly components (of equal quality), produce with lower wage rates, eliminate product features (costs) not valued by customers
  - Outsource production to reduce product cost and/or inventories the company must carry on its balance sheet
  - Reduce raw materials inventories via just-in-time deliveries
  - Eliminate bottlenecks in manufacturing to reduce work-in-process inventories
  - Reduce finished goods inventories by producing to order rather than producing to estimated demand
- Increase payables
  - Extend the time for payment of low or no-cost payables—so long as the relationship with suppliers is not harmed)

b. The terms of payment that a company offers to its customers is a marketing tool, similar to product price and advertising programs. Many companies promote payment terms separately from other promotions (no payment for six months or interest free financing, for example). As companies restrict credit terms, the level of receivables will likely decrease, thereby reducing working capital. The restriction of credit terms may also have the undesirable effect of reducing demand for the company's products. The cost of credit terms must be weighed against the benefits, and credit terms must be managed with care so as to optimize costs rather than minimize them. Credit policy is as much art as it is science.

C4-48—continued

Likewise, the depth and breadth of the inventories that companies carry impact customer perception. At the extreme, inventory stock-outs result in not only the loss of current sales, but also the potential loss of future sales as customers are introduced to competitors and may develop an impression of the company as "thinly stocked." Inventories are costly to maintain, as they must be financed, insured, stocked, moved, and so forth. Reduction in inventory levels can reduce these costs. On the other hand, the amount and type of inventories carried is a marketing decision and must be managed with care so as to optimize the level inventories, not necessarily to minimize them.

One company's account payable is another's account receivable. So, just as one company seeks to extend the time of payment, so as to reduce its working capital, so does the other company seek to reduce the average collection period so as to accomplish the same objective. Capable, dependable suppliers are a valuable resource for the company, and the supplier relation must be handled with care. All companies take as long to pay their accounts payable as the supplier allows in its credit terms. Extending the payment terms beyond that point begins to negatively impact the supplier relation, ultimately resulting in the loss of the supplier. The supplier relation must be managed with care so as to optimize the terms of payment, rather than necessarily to minimize them.

Financial Accounting for MBAs, 3rd Edition

Module 5

Reporting and Analyzing Operating Income

QUESTIONS

Q5-2. Financial statement analysis is usually conducted for purposes of forecasting future financial performance of the company. Extraordinary items are, by definition, not expected to continue to affect the profits and cash flows of the company. Accordingly, the financial statements separately report extraordinary items from continuing operations to yield an income measure that is more likely to persist into the future.

Q5-4. *Basic* earnings per share utilizes reported net income and common shares outstanding in its computation. *Diluted* earnings per share includes the effects of dilutive securities, assuming that they are exercised at the beginning of the year (or when issued if issued during the year). The numerator, thus, adds back preferred dividends and forgone interest expense on convertible debt. The denominator reflects the additional common shares assumed to be issued upon conversion of convertible securities or upon the exercise of options.

Securities cannot be included in the diluted EPS computation if they are *antidilutive*. Antidilutive securities are those that cause an increase, rather than a decrease in basic EPS. An example is employee stock options whose exercise price exceeds the current market price (underwater or out-of-the-money options).

Q5-6. Restructuring costs consist of two general categories: *asset write-downs* and *liability accruals*. Asset write-downs reduce assets' net book value and are recognized in the income statement as an expense. Liability accruals create a liability, such as for anticipated severance costs and exit costs, and yield a corresponding expense that reduces income and equity.

Big bath refers to a companies' overestimating the amount of asset write-downs or liability accruals to deliberately reduce current period earnings so as to remove future expenses from the balance sheet. Big baths create 'reserves' that can be used to increase future period earnings.

Q5-8. Deferred tax liabilities generally result from the recognition of expense (most typically depreciation expense) earlier in the tax return than in the financial reporting income statement. If no other depreciable assets are acquired, future taxable income will be higher and the company will have to pay more taxes (a

©Cambridge Business Publishers, 2008

future tax liability). However, if the company acquires additional depreciable assets, the company will continue to deduct initial years' accelerated depreciation and the future taxes will be permanently avoided. If the asset growth is sufficiently high, the tax liability can be deferred indefinitely. If the asset growth subsequently declines, however, such as resulting from a downsizing of the business, or a business downturn, the deferred tax liability will likely result in a real cash outflow.

Q5-10. Unearned revenue is cash a company receives from customers but has not yet earned. Until the company earns the revenue it is a liability. If the company expects to earn the revenue in the coming year, it is a current liability; otherwise, it's a long-term liability. Examples of unearned revenue include: customer deposits, gift cards, season tickets, membership fees, partial payments in advance, and lay-away plans of retailers.

MINI EXERCISES

M5-12 Bartov Corporation

		Balance Sheet					Income Statement		
Transaction	Cash Asset	+ Noncash Assets	= Liabil-ities	+ Contrib Capital	+ Earned Capital		Rev-enues	− Expen-ses	= Net Income
2005: Record $400,000 construction costs	−400,000 Cash		=		−400,000 Retained Earnings			+400,000 Cost of Sales	= −400,000
2005: Recognize $525,000 revenue for contract		+525,000 Accounts Receivable	=		+525,00 Retained Earnings		+525,000 Revenue	−	= +525,000
2006: Record $1,000,000 construction costs	−1,000,000 Cash		=		−1,000,000 Retained Earnings			+1,000,000 Cost of Sales	= −1,000,000
2006: Recognize $1,325,000 revenue for contract		+1,325,000 Accounts Receivable	=		+1,325,000 Retained Earnings		+1,325,000 Revenues	−	= +1,325,000
2007: Record $500,000 construction costs	−500,000 Cash		=		−500,000 Retained Earnings			+500,000 Cost of Sales	= −500,000
2007: Recognize $650,000 revenue for completed contract		+650,000 Accounts Receivable	=		+650,00 Retained Earnings		+650,000 Revenues	−	= +650,000

Left margin journal entries:

```
OGS   400,000
   Cash   400,000

      COGS
400,000|

      Cash
         |400,000

AR    525,000
   Rev   525,000
      AR
525,000|

      Rev
         |525,000

COGS 1,000,000
   Cash 1,000,000
      COGS
1,000,000|

      Cash
         |1,000,000

AR  1,325,000
   Rev  1,325,000
      AR
1,325,000|

      Rev
         |1,325,000

COGS 500,000
   Cash 500,000
      COGS
500,000|

      Cash
         |500,000

AR    650,000
   Rev   650,000
      AR
650,000|

      Rev
         |650,000
```

M5-14 (15 minutes)

Two potential revenue recognition problems for a company with operations similar to BannerAD follow:

1. Sales on consignment: BannerAD earns revenue as an agent for the seller. It does not take title to the inventory and, as a result, cannot characterize the gross revenues as sales. Rather, it should disclose the consignment arrangement and identify its revenues as commissions rather than sales. Thus, one potential problem could arise if BannerAd records these commissions before the sale is actually made to the final buyer.

2. Gross vs. Net: Many dotcom's recorded commission sales at gross amount, rather than the net commission that represented the true earnings for the agent on the sale of the inventory. Grossing up the sales inflates top line growth, often a key indicator of Internet site value.

M5-16 (10 minutes)

a. $1,821 / $22,338 = 8.2%. To assess Abbott's R&D expenditure level, we would gather R&D expenditure data for Abbott's competitors to gain a sense of the appropriateness of Abbott's R&D expenditures. As well, we could gather information about R&D spending for all public companies to assess whether economy-wide factors are at play.

b. Under current U.S. GAAP, all R&D costs must be expensed when incurred. This policy applies to depreciable assets that would otherwise be capitalized, unless the assets have alternative future uses. As a result, the balance sheet does not reflect the costs incurred for long-term R&D assets. In addition, under current GAAP, operating expenses are increased, retained earnings are reduced and thus stockholders' equity is lower.

M5-18 (15 minutes)

a. Cisco reports $2,295 million of tax expense in its income statement. This is the total of Federal, state and foreign taxes.

b. The current portion is $2,240 million ($1,340 + $496 million + $404 million).

c. Companies maintain two set of books. One is maintained in conformity with GAAP and is used to prepare publicly available financial statements. The other is maintained in conformity with tax regulations, and is used to prepare the company's tax return. Timing differences frequently arise between the two in the recognition of revenues and expenses. That is, although the same total revenues and expense will ultimately be recognized, they are recognized in different periods. Deferred tax liabilities and assets reflect future tax expense and deductions, respectively. As deferred tax liabilities (assets) increase, reported tax expense increases (decreases), and as deferred tax liabilities (assets) decrease, reported tax expense decreases (increases).

M5-20 (20 minutes)

a. Koonce should record one-sixth of the season ticket receipts (or $70,000) after each production.

b.

		Balance Sheet					Income Statement		
Transaction	Cash Asset	+ Noncash Assets	= Liabil- ities	+ Contrib Capital	+ Earned Capital		Rev- enues	− Expen- ses	= Net Income
Receive cash in advance for season tickets	+420,000 Cash		+420,000 = Unearned Revenue					−	=
Recognize revenue for first production			−70,000 = Unearned Revenue		+70,000 Retained Earnings		+70,000 Revenues	−	= +70,000

sh 420,000
UR   420,000

Cash
420,000|

UR
        |420,000

70,000
Rev   70,000

UR
70,000|

Rev
        |70,000

EXERCISES

E5-22 (20 minutes)

Company	Revenue recognition
The Limited	When the customer takes the merchandise and the right of return period has expired.
Boeing Corporation	Revenue is recognized under long-term contracts under the percentage-of-completion method.
Supervalu	When the customer takes the merchandise and cash is received.
MTV	When the content is aired by the TV stations
Real estate developer	When title to the houses is transferred to the buyers.
Bank of America	Interest is earned by the passage of time. Each period, Bank of America accrues income on each of its loans and establishes an account receivable on its balance sheet.
Harley-Davidson	When title to the motorcycles is transferred to the buyer. Harley will also set up a reserve for anticipated warranty costs and recognize the expected warranty cost expense when it recognizes the sales revenue.
Time-Warner	When the magazines are sent to subscribers. Subscriptions received in advance are deferred revenue (a liability) until the magazines are mailed.

E5-24 (20 minutes)

a.

($ millions)		Percentage-of-Completion Method			Completed Contract	
Year	Costs incurred	Percent of total expected costs	Revenue recognized (percentage of costs incurred × total contract amount)	Income (revenue – costs incurred)	Revenue recognized	Income
2006	$100	25%	$125	$ 25	$ 0	$ 0
2007	300	75%	375	75	500	100
	$400		$500	$100	$500	$100

b. The percentage-of-completion method normally provides a reasonable estimate of the revenues, expenses, and income earned for each period. A key is obtaining good estimates of expected costs and costs to date. This method is also acceptable under GAAP for contracts spanning more than one accounting period.

E5-26 (20 minutes)

a. FedEx reports income tax expense of $864 million in 2005, $481 million in 2004, and $508 million in 2003.

b. We can calculate the percentage currently payable by dividing the current provision by total tax expense. This yields 93% ($802 million / $864 million) in 2005, 106% ($510 million / $481 million) in 2004, and 35% ($179 million / $508 million) in 2003. The amount of income tax currently payable fluctuates greatly from 2003 to 2005. This is due to fluctuations in the amount of deferred taxes, from a deferred tax benefit of $29 million in 2004 to a deferred tax expense of $329 million in 2003. These arise because the rules differ for computing financial reporting income versus taxable income.

c. Deferred tax liabilities increase when the net book value of assets reported for tax purposes is less than that for financial reporting purposes. The most common reason this occurs is because firms use an accelerated depreciation method for tax purposes that results in a lower net book value of assets on the tax books in the earlier years of the asset's life vis-à-vis the net book value on the financial accounting books (that reflect straight-line depreciation for GAAP purposes).

E5-28 (20 minutes)

a. The following items are operating: net sales and revenues, cost of sales, research and development expenses, selling, administrative and general expenses, health care claims and costs, other operating expenses, and taxes on operating profit. Equity in income of unconsolidated affiliates relates to Deere's investments in companies over which it exerts significant influence, but does not control. This income is viewed as operating so long as the related investment is considered an operating asset. In Deere's income statement, only interest expense would be viewed as nonoperating.

b. Of particular interest is the categorization of Deere's finance and interest income and its health care premiums and fees. Deere's financial services business segment provides loans and leases for equipment sold to dealers as well as purchasing end-customer receivables from those dealers. The financing activities can, thus, be viewed as an extension of the sales process, quite unlike the investment in marketable securities unrelated to the company's activities. These captive finance operations are generally viewed as operating.

Similarly, Deere's health care operations provide managed health care services for the company and some of its customers. This is a business line, just as is equipment sales. It can, therefore, also be viewed as an operating activity.

E5-30 (20 minutes)

a. R&D as a percent of sales

	AMD	INTC
2003	24.2%	14.5%
2004	18.7%	14.0%
2005	19.6%	13.3%

b. R&D costs are expensed in the income statement, except for the portion relating to depreciable assets that have alternate uses. Expensing of R&D expenses (rather than capitalizing and depreciating them) reduces assets on both AMC and INTC's balance sheets. As well, expensing R&D expenses as incurred increases expense which reduces profit reported on the income statement and stockholders' equity on the balance sheet (via the reduction in retained earnings).

c. It is very difficult to evaluate the effectiveness of R&D. To the extent that companies can realize economies of scale, INTC's lower R&D spending as a percent of sales does not necessarily indicate that it places less importance on this activity. Further, R&D spending affects revenues but with some time lag (current period R&D expenditures yield future sales). Over time, however, the number and quality of new product introductions, number of patents, etc., can be compared across companies and against relative levels of R&D spending.

E5-32 (25 minutes)

a. Barnes & Noble receives cash for year-long memberships throughout the year. When it receives the $25 cash from a customer, the company records it as a current liability. Then, Barnes & Noble recognizes revenue over the year so that, by the time the membership expires, the company has recorded the entire membership fee as revenue. Barnes & Noble does not recognize the revenue evenly over the year, but rather based on historic sales patterns. For example, the company likely has higher sales during the holiday season and, so, recognizes more of the membership fees as revenue then.

b. When Barnes & Noble receives the cash it increases a current liability called deferred revenue or unearned membership fees. This is a current liability on the balance sheet because the membership only lasts a year.

c. The discount is not recorded at the time the membership fees are received. Each time a member makes a purchase, the company records 10% less revenue that if a non-member made the same purchase. This does not affect the balance sheet.

P5-34 (30 minutes)

a. "Deferred tax liabilities" are items for which the company has received a tax deduction, but that have not yet been recorded in the income statement. "Deferred tax assets" are items that have been recorded in the income statement, but can be used as a tax deduction or credit in future periods. Both of these relate to temporary timing differences between the income statement prepared under GAAP and the tax return prepared under tax regulations. An example of a deferred tax liability is the use of accelerated depreciation for tax purposes and straight-line for the GAAP income statement. An example of a deferred tax asset is the accrual of severance expense under a restructuring program for the GAAP income statement that will not become a tax deduction until paid.

b. The deferred tax liability relating to intangibles is similar to that for depreciable assets like buildings and equipment. In this case, Pfizer has acquired intangible assets in the purchase of a company and it is amortizing the intangibles (the term used for the depreciation of an intangible asset) more quickly for tax purposes than for financial-reporting purposes. Thus, the book value in financial reporting books is greater than on the tax books. Eventually, the amortization expense in its tax return will become smaller than that in its GAAP income statement, resulting in higher taxable income and tax payment liability. It is this liability for future taxes that is being recorded as the deferred tax liability on the balance sheet.

c. Those plans for which Pfizer is recording expenses more quickly for its GAAP income statement than for its tax returns are generating deferred tax assets. Those plans for which Pfizer is recognizing tax deductions more quickly than it is recording expenses in its GAAP income statements are generating deferred tax liabilities.

d. The deferred tax liability for un-remitted earnings relates to an investment in one or more affiliates for which Pfizer is recording income, but has not yet received cash. Un-remitted means that the affiliate has recognized income (which Pfizer has recorded in its financial reporting books), but has not yet paid out that profit to shareholders (including Pfizer) as a dividend. The deferred tax liability tells you that Pfizer has recorded income without the receipt of cash. Further, if and when the affiliate pays a dividend, Pfizer will have to pay taxes on the dividend when received.

P5-34 (continued)

e. Operating loss carryforwards arise when a company reports a loss in its tax return. It can carry that loss back for up to 2 years to offset against taxable income and receive a tax refund. Unused tax losses can be carried forward for up to 20 years as future tax deductions to reduce future taxable income and taxes payable. This benefit is an asset to the company.

f. The deferred tax asset valuation allowance arises when the company believes that some of its deferred tax assets will not generate a future tax benefit. These allowances typically relate to loss carryforward deferred tax assets that the company believes will expire unused. Increases and decreases in deferred tax valuation allowances affect net income dollar-for-dollar. In this case, Pfizer's net income has been reduced cumulatively by $142 million. During 2005, the valuation allowance decreased by $35. This decreased tax expense by $35 and increased 2005 net income by the same amount.

P5-36 (30 minutes)

a. FedEx reports $864 million of tax expense in its 2005 income statement. Of this amount, $802 is currently payable.

b. Deferred tax liabilities relating to PPE arise because FDX is depreciating buildings and equipment (land is not a depreciable asset) more quickly in its tax return than for its GAAP income statement. Thus, the assets' tax-reporting book value is less than the financial-reporting book value, which yields a deferred tax liability. For any particular asset, future depreciation expense in the tax return will be lower and the difference between the two net book values will shrink and the liability will reverse. However, if Fedex adds significant depreciable assets each year, the first-year's accelerated depreciation on the new assets will more than offset the lower depreciation on the older assets, resulting in a permanent deferred tax liability. Once the growth rate for assets subsides, the depreciation expense deduction in the tax return will as well, and the deferred tax liability will shrink.

a. Fedex reports an accrued liability for self-insurance on its balance sheet. This does not create a tax-basis liability however because this sort of expense is not deductible until paid. Consequently, GAAP liabilities are greater than tax-basis liabilities and this results in a deferred tax asset that recognizes the future deductions of the self-insurance payments.

b. Operating loss carryforwards arise when a company reports a tax loss, which it can carry back for up to 2 years to offset against taxable income

©Cambridge Business Publishers, 2008

and receive a tax refund. Unused tax losses can be carried forward for up to 20 years as future tax deductions to reduce future taxable income and tax liability. This creates a deferred tax asset.

c. The valuation allowance arises when the company believes that some of the related deferred tax assets will not generate future benefits. These allowances typically arise because the carryforward deduction will likely not be used before it expires. Increases and decreases in deferred tax valuation allowances affect net income dollar-for-dollar. FedEx's net income has been reduced cumulatively by $42 million. For 2005, the decrease in the allowance, increased net income by $10 million. Since establishing and subsequently adjusting the valuation allowance is highly subjective (dependent upon the company's estimation of whether the deductions will or will not be realized), companies might increase or decrease this account to manage net income to reach income targets. Financial statement users need to be aware of how changes in the valuation allowance affects net income in their analysis of the profitability of the company.

P5-38 (30 minutes)

a. In 2001, DJ recorded a restructuring cost relating to abandoned lease space. The decision to abandon the leased space necessitated an accrual of $32.2 million. Specifically, DJ recorded a liability on its balance sheet and a related expense on its income statement.

In 2004, DJ decided to re-occupy a portion of the leased premise. Since this space was no longer "abandoned," the company reversed $2.761 million of the original $32.2 million accrual. This reversal had two effects: first, the liability on the balance sheet was reduced; second, the related expense was reversed. The latter produced income (negative expense) in 2004, the year of the reversal. Since the additional income is a one-time event, the $2.761 million should not be factored into projections of future operating results.

b. In 2005, DJ recorded a restructuring charge of $11.4 million relating to expected severance of employees. Following approval by its board of directors regarding management's decision to terminate these employees, DJ recorded the effects of the decision by recording a liability on the balance sheet and an expense on the income statement for $11.4 million.

Of the $11.4 million liability initially recorded, $6.8 million was paid in 2005, resulting in a remaining liability of $4.6 million at the end of 2005. Presumably, DJ will pay the remaining severance costs in 2006 and thereafter.

P5-40 (40 minutes)

a. i. Altria received 430 million shares of SABMiller valued at approximately $3.4 billion, based upon a share price of 5.12 British pounds per share.

   ii. The book value of Altria's investment in Miller on the date of sale can be computed as: VALUE RECEIVED – BOOK VALUE = PRE-TAX GAIN OR LOSS. Substituting the numbers, we get:

$3.4 billion – $___?___ = $2.6 billion
$3.4 billion – $0.8 billion = $2.6 billion

   iii. Altria recorded a pre-tax gain of $2.6 billion and an after-tax gain of $1.7 billion related to the SABMiller transaction.

b. Altria received none of the purchase price in cash. The proceeds received were in the form of SABMiller common stock.

c. This sale is a one-time event and the resulting gain should, therefore, be considered as a transitory item for analysis purposes.

   Moreover, the cash flows related to Miller Brewing will no longer be a component of Altria's future cash flows. Altria will potentially receive future cash flows related to its ownership of stock in the purchasing company (SABMiller), either in the form of dividends or from the sale of SABMiller stock, or both.

P5-42 (40 minutes)

a. If Centex does not close a sale, it records the $1,000 customer deposit as deferred revenue, a current liability. Signing up customers is not how Centex earns revenue—it earns revenue by building the home and getting the customer's final acceptance. Therefore, deposits are not revenue when they are received.

b. At the end of March 2006, Centex' balance sheet has a current liability for the deposits on the backlog units. At $1,000 a unit, this liability totals $17,387,000.

c. Centex likely uses a percentage of completion method to record revenue. Therefore, Centex will record the deposits on the backlog units as revenue when the company begins to construct the home and incurs construction costs. The company will not receive the full price of the home (nor record it as revenue) until all construction is complete, the home passes government inspection, and the customer signs off on the contract. In the interim, the company will use the percentage-of-completion method to recognize revenues.

d. When Centex refunds a deposit to a customer, it reduces both cash and the deferred revenue liability.

©Cambridge Business Publishers, 2008

CASES

C5-44 (30 minutes)

a. The SEC's position (SAB 101) is that if the company's practice is to obtain sales authorization, revenue is *not* recognized until such approval is obtained, even though product delivery is made and approval by the customer is anticipated. The language from SAB 101 is as follows: "Generally the staff believes that, in view of [the company's] business practice of requiring a written sales agreement for this class of customer, persuasive evidence of an arrangement would require a final agreement that has been executed by the properly authorized personnel of the customer. In the staff's view, [the customer's] execution of the sales agreement after the end of the quarter causes the transaction to be considered a transaction of the subsequent period. Further, if an arrangement is subject to subsequent approval (*e.g.*, by the management committee or board of directors) or execution of another agreement, revenue recognition would be inappropriate until that subsequent approval or agreement is complete."

b. The sales commission will be larger because of the sale. This might motivate management's decision. Alternatively, perhaps management feels that the sales (and profit) increase will drive up the company's stock price. The parties benefiting from this action include the salesperson and, potentially, the company, its shareholders, management, other employees, and etc. There are parties that are adversely affected by this action, however. These include future shareholders and short-sellers of the company's stock (who sell overvalued stock), the company's auditors, suppliers, and current and future employees.

c. Corporate governance involves policies and procedures that protect the assets of the company, and protect the company and its stakeholders from unauthorized actions. These controls include a code of conduct, a clear set of operating procedures, and an effective audit function to ensure that those procedures are followed. The Board of Directors has a fiduciary responsibility to the shareholders, and a legal responsibility under the Sarbanes-Oxley Act, to establish and maintain an effective corporate governance system. Review procedures should be in place requiring officers to attest that requisite approvals have been obtained, and all other conditions of the sale fulfilled, before revenue can be recognized.

Module 6

Reporting and Analyzing Operating Assets

QUESTIONS

Q6-2. If inventory costs are stable, the per unit dollar cost of inventories (beginning or ending) tends to be approximately the same under different inventory costing methods and the choice of method does not materially affect net income. To see this, remember that FIFO profits include holding gains on inventories. If the inflation rate is low (or inventories turn quickly), there will be less holding gains (inflationary profit) in inventory.

Q6-4. If inventory costs are rising, (a) Last-in, first-out yields the lowest ending inventory (b) Last-in, first-out yields the lowest net income, (c) First-in, first-out yields the highest ending inventory, (d) First-in, first-out yields the highest net income, (e) Last in, first-out yields the highest cash flow because taxes are lowest.

Q6-6. Kaiser Aluminum Corporation is using the lower of cost or market (LCM) rule. When the replacement cost for inventory falls below its (FIFO or LIFO) historical cost, the inventory must be written down to its replacement cost (market value).

Q6-8. When a company revises its estimate of an asset's useful life or its salvage value, depreciation expense is recalculated. One way is to depreciate the current undepreciated cost of the asset (original cost – accumulated depreciation) using the revised assumptions of remaining useful life and salvage value.

Q6-10. The primary benefit of accelerated depreciation for tax reporting is that the higher depreciation deductions in the early years of the asset's life reduce taxable income and income taxes. This increases cash flow that can be invested to yield additional cash inflows (e.g., an "interest-free loan" that can be used to generate additional income). We would generally prefer to receive cash inflows sooner rather than later in order to maximize this investment potential.

MINI EXERCISES

M 6-12 (10 minutes)

a. To bring the allowance from $500 to the desired balance of $2,100, the company will need to increase the allowance account by **$1,600**, resulting in bad debt expense of that same amount.

b. The net amount of Accounts Receivable reported in current assets is calculated as follows: $98,000 – $2,100 = **$95,900**.

M 6-14 (20 minutes)

a.

($ millions)	2005	2004
Accounts receivable (net)...............................	$3,385	$3,541
Allowance for uncollectible accounts..........	92	118
Gross accounts receivable............................	$3,477	$3,659
Percentage of uncollectible accounts to gross accounts receivable..........................	2.65% ($92 / $3,477)	3.22% ($118 / $3,659)

b. The reduction in the allowance for uncollectible accounts as a percentage of gross accounts receivable is very slight. Nonetheless, the dip may indicate that the quality of the accounts receivable has improved, perhaps because the economy has improved, the company is selling to a more creditworthy class of customers, or the company's management of accounts receivable has improved. It may also indicate, however, that the receivables are under-reserved (e.g., allowance account is too low). This would result in higher reported profits in the current year at the expense of future profits when the allowance for uncollectible accounts is increased.

M 6-16 (20 minutes)

a. FIFO cost of goods sold = 1,000 @ $100 + 700 @ $150 = $205,000
   FIFO ending inventories = $400,000 - $205,000 = $195,000

b. LIFO cost of goods sold = 1,700 @ $150 = $255,000
   LIFO ending inventories = $400,000 - $255,000 = $145,000

c. AC cost of goods sold = 1,700 @ $400,000 / 3,000 = $226,667
   AC ending inventories = $400,000 – $226,667 = $173,333

M 6-18 (20 minutes)

a.

	Inventory Turnover rates for 2006
ANF..	$933 / [($211 + $363) / 2] = 3.25
TJX	$12,295 / [($2,352+$2,366) / 2] = 5.21

b. TJX' inventory turnover rate is higher than ANF's. TJX concentrates on the value-priced end of the clothing spectrum. Thus, it realizes a lower profit margin that must be offset with higher turnover in order to yield an acceptable return on net operating assets (see discussion of profitability and turnover in Module 4).

c. Inventory turnover improves as the volume of goods sold increases relative to the dollar value of goods on hand. Retailers must balance the cost savings from inventory reductions against the marketing implications of lower inventory levels on hand. Companies can lower inventory levels by reducing the depth and breadth of product lines carried (e.g., not carrying every style, size and color), eliminating slow-moving product lines, working with suppliers to arrange for delivery when needed, and marking down goods for sale at the end of product seasons.

M 6-20 (15 minutes)

a. Straight-line depreciation

2007:   ($145,800 - $5,400) x (8/36) = $31,200

2008:   ($145,800 - $5,400) x (12/36) = $46,800

b. Double-declining-balance depreciation
Preliminary computation: Twice straight-line rate = 2/3 = 66⅔%

2007:   ($145,800 x 66⅔%) x (8/12) = $64,800

2008:   ($145,800 - $64,800) x 66⅔% = $54,000

EXERCISES

E 6-22 (20 minutes)

a. 2007 bad debts expense computation

$90,000 × 1%	=	$	900
20,000 × 2%	=		400
11,000 × 5%	=		550
6,000 × 10%	=		600
4,000 × 25%	=		1,000
			$3,450

Less: Unused balance before adjustment 520

Bad debt expense for 2007 .... $2,930

b.

BDE 2,930
  AU 2,930

	BDE	
2,930		

	AU	
		2,930

Transaction	Balance Sheet					Income Statement		
	Cash Asset	+ Noncash Assets	= Liabil- ities	+ Contrib. Capital	+ Earned Capital	Rev- enues	– Expen- ses	= Net Income
2007: Record bad debt expense		-2,930 Allowance for Uncollectible Accounts =			-2,930 Retained Earnings		+2,930 – Bad Debt Expense =	-2,930

c. Accounts receivable, net = $131,000 - $3,450 = $127,550

Reported in the balance sheet as follows:

Accounts receivable, net of allowance of $3,450 .... $127,550

E 6-24 (25 minutes)

a,b.

($ millions)	2005	2004
Accounts receivable (net)	$ 9,903	$10,226
Allowance for uncollectible accounts	227	286
Gross accounts receivable........................	$10,130	$10,512
Percentage of uncollectible accounts to gross accounts receivable	2.24% ($227/$10,130)	2.72% ($286/$10,512)

c.

($ millions)	2005	2004	2003
Bad debt expense (reversal of allowance)	$17	$(6)	$29
Amounts actually written off	$76	$64	$92

The provision (increase in the allowance account arising from bad debt expense recorded on the income statement) has generally declined from 2003 to 2005, and was even a negative amount in 2004 (i.e. bad debt expense increased net income in 2004). The receivables that the company wrote off, exhibit a similar pattern.

d. The allowance for uncollectible accounts has decreased as a percentage of gross accounts receivable from 2.72% in 2004 to 2.24% in 2005 (see part b). In 2004, HP allowed its allowance account to decline as a percentage of gross accounts receivable as the provision was actually reversed, resulting in negative bad debt expense (increase in profitability). One way to gauge the adequacy of the allowance account is to look at write-offs as a percentage of the allowance account at the beginning of the year. In 2004, this percentage is 18.4% ($64/$347) and for 2005 it is 26.6% ($76/$286). HP's write-offs as a percentage of the allowance increased from 2004 to 2005. This means that the bad debt expense is not keeping up with actual accounts that go bad. As well, HP has a smaller allowance account in 2005 compared to 2004 (although sales *are* dropping). If HP's allowance was adequate in 2003, the reversal in 2004 (with the consequent increase in profitability in that year) appears to have been more than necessary. Further insight might be gained by comparing HP's accounts to those of its peers.

E6-26 (30 minutes)

a.

Year	Sales	Collections	Accounts Written Off	Acc Recble. Balance
2005	$751,000	$733,000	$5,300	$12,700
2006	876,000	864,000	5,800	18,900
2007	972,000	938,000	6,500	46,400
Total	$2,599,000	$2,535,000	$17,600	

Uncollectible Accounts Expense is:

2005	$ 7,510	computed as 1% × $751,000
2006	8,760	computed as 1% × $876,000
2007	9,720	computed as 1% × $972,000
2005–2007	$25,990	computed as 1% × $2,599,000

Allowance for Uncollectible Accounts is:
$8,390, computed as $25,990 total provision for uncollectible accounts less $17,600 in total write-offs.

b.   The 1% rate appears to be too high. A 0.8% rate would have provided $20,792, which still exceeds the $17,600 total write-off by $3,192. Moreover, this smaller allowance seems large enough to provide an adequate margin for future write-offs.

E6-28 (25 minutes)

a. GE's balance sheet reports $10,315, which is the LIFO inventory value.

b. GE's balance sheet would have reported $11,012, which is FIFO inventory value.

c. Pretax income has been reduced by $697 million ($11,012 million - $10,315 million) cumulatively since GE adopted LIFO inventory costing. This is because it has matched current inventory costs against current selling prices, thus avoiding the recognition of holding gains that would have resulted had FIFO inventory costing been used.

d. Pretax income has been reduced by $697 million (see part c). Assuming a 35% tax rate, taxes have been reduced by $697 x 0.35 = $244 million.

Cumulative taxes have been decreased by the use of LIFO inventory costing.

e. For 2005, the LIFO reserve increased by $36 million ($697 million - $661 million). Pretax income has been reduced by this amount, relative to the FIFO method, thus reducing taxes by $36 million x 0.35 = $12.6 million.

E6-30 (25 minutes)

a. Deere reports $2,135 million for inventories on its 2005 balance sheet. (Its 2004 inventories are $1,999 million.)

b. Had Deere used FIFO method, its balance sheet would have reported $3,267 million as inventories. (Its 2004 inventories would have been $3,001 million.)

c. Pretax income has been decreased by $1,132 million cumulatively since Deere adopted LIFO inventory costing ($3,267 - $2,135). This decline occurs because Deere has matched current inventory costs against current selling prices, which are higher than the older costs in ending inventory because prices have been rising.

d. Pretax income has been decreased by $1,132 million (see part c). Assuming a 35% tax rate, cumulative taxes were lower by $1,132 x 0.35 = $396.2 million as compared to the taxes that Deere would have paid had it used the FIFO system. (As of 2004, its cumulative taxes were lower by $350.7 million.)

e. For 2005, the change in the LIFO reserve is an increase of $130 million ($1,132 million - $1,002 million). This reduces pretax income by that amount (as compared to the taxable income that Deere would have reported had it used the FIFO system). Assuming a tax rate of 35%, Deere saved taxes of $130 million x 0.35 = $45.5 million in 2005 because it used the LIFO costing method.

E6-32 (25 minutes)

a. 1. Cumulative depreciation expense to date of sale:
   [($800,000-$80,000) / 10 years] x 6 years = $432,000

   2. Net book value of the plane at date of sale:
   $800,000 - $432,000 = $368,000

b. 1. There is no gain or loss if the cash proceeds are equal to the net book value.

   2. Loss on sale of: $195,000 - $368,000 = $173,000

   3. Gain on sale of: $600,000 - $368,000 = $232,000

E6-34 (20 minutes)

a. Depreciation expense to date of sale is [($27,200-$2,000) / 6] per year x 3 years =$12,600.

   The net book value of the van is, therefore, $27,200-$12,600=$14,600.

b. 1.There is no gain or loss if the cash proceeds are equal to the net book value.

   2. $400 gain ($15,000 - $14,600)

   3. $2,600 loss ($12,000 - $14,600)

E 6-36 (25 minutes)

a.

	Receivable turnover rate	Inventory turnover rate	PPE turnover rate
2004	$\dfrac{\$20,011}{\frac{\$2,714+\$2,792}{2}} = 7.27$	$\dfrac{\$9,958}{\frac{\$1,816+\$1,897}{2}} = 5.36$	$\dfrac{\$20,011}{\frac{\$5,609+\$5,711}{2}} = 3.54$
2005	$\dfrac{\$21,167}{\frac{\$2,792+\$2,838}{2}} = 7.52$	$\dfrac{\$10,381}{\frac{\$1,897+\$2,162}{2}} = 5.12$	$\dfrac{\$21,167}{\frac{\$5,711+\$5,593}{2}} = 3.75$

b. 3M has improved its receivables and PPE turnover rates, but its inventory turnover rate has fallen. Receivable turnover rates can be improved by monitoring more closely the quality of customers to which credit is granted, implementing better collection procedures, and offering discounts as an incentive for early payment. Inventory turnover rates can be improved by weeding out slow-moving product lines, by reducing the depth and breadth of products carried, and by implementing just-in-time deliveries. PPE turns can be improved by off-loading manufacturing to other companies in the supply chain and acquiring long-term operating assets in partnership with other companies, say in a joint venture.

PROBLEMS

P6-38 (30 minutes)

a. Best Buy and Sharper Image, both retailers, report much higher receivables turnover rates than do the manufacturers, Caterpillar and Harley. The likely reason for this is that retail sales are usually via cash, check, or credit cards (which are like cash for the retailers). Recall that the turnover ratio includes credit sales but because most firms do not report credit sales, the turnover ratio uses total sales. Manufacturers, on the other hand, usually sell to retailers on credit and the accounts are not collected for a much longer period of time. CAT and HDI both have finance subsidiaries that provide loan and lease financing. The longer term of these receivables reduces turnover rates.

b. Harley's relatively higher inventory turnover rate, compared with retailer, Sharper Image, is surprising as manufacturers typically turn their inventories much more slowly than do retailers. There are at least two possible reasons for Harley's low inventory levels relative to cost of goods sold: i) Harley has a very efficient manufacturing process that minimizes raw materials and work-in-process inventories, and/or ii) demand is high for Harley's products and the motorcycles are sold before production begins, thus minimizing finished goods inventories.

Oracle is a software development and service company and does not carry inventories of products for sale.

c. Carnival, the cruise ship line, is capital-intensive. Microsoft, on the other hand, requires relatively few PPE assets to support its operations. Microsoft's R&D costs are expensed under GAAP rather than capitalized as PPE. Thus, Microsoft's PPE turnover is much higher than Carnival's.

d. The relative asset turnover rates reported generally conform to our expectations across industries. Those industries that sell on credit, rather than using credit cards, or that normally stock inventories for production and sale, or that require substantial investment in long-term assets yield much lower receivable, inventory, and PPE turnover rates respectively. These lower turnover rates must be accompanied by higher profit margins and/or higher financial leverage so as to yield a satisfactory return on net operating assets. Generally, we expect the following:

Industry	Receivables TO	Inventory TO	PPE TO
Retailing.................	↑	↑	↑
Manufacturing	↓	↓	↓

P6-40 (40 minutes)

(all in $ thousands consistent with Intuit's financial statements)

a. Gross receivables as of 2005 are $86,125 + $15,653 = $101,778.
   Gross receivables as of 2004 are $81,615 + $6,994 = $88,609.

b. Estimated uncollectible accounts as a percentage of gross accounts receivable are:
   15.4% ($15,653 / $101,778) in 2005
   7.9% ($6,994 / $88,609) in 2004

   The allowance for uncollectible accounts has nearly doubled as a percentage of gross accounts receivable. This could be because there is greater uncertainty about the collectibility of receivables in general, or one or more significant accounts are in arrears.

c. The receivables turnover rate is $\dfrac{\$2,038,000}{\dfrac{\$101,778 + \$88,609}{2}} = 21.41$

   Average collection period (days sales in accounts receivable) is:
   $101,778 / ($2,038,000 / 365) = <u>18.23 days</u>

   Intuit's sales to consumers are primarily via on-line purchases using credit cards for payment. The days sales in accounts receivables will, therefore, be low for this portion of its business. Service revenues are likely on account, and the collection period is likely to be longer for this segment of Intuit's business. The overall days sales in accounts receivable is an average of these lines of business.

d. Intuit substantially increased its allowance for uncollectible accounts as a percentage of gross accounts receivable. There are two possible reasons for this, neither of which are particularly favorable:

   1. The financial condition of one or more customers has deteriorated markedly, thus warranting a higher reserve, or

   2. Intuit arbitrarily increased its allowance account to create a reserve that it can use in future periods to inflate earnings.

e. Intuit's allowance for uncollectible accounts is increased by the provision ("additions charged to expense") and is decreased by write-offs of accounts receivable ("deductions"). Over the three-year period covered by the table, INTU has increased its allowance account by a cumulative amount of $20,550 ($1,410 + $5,325 + $13,815). It has written off a cumulative total of $10,432 ($1,850 + $3,426 + $5,156). The allowance account has, therefore, increased by $10,118 ($20,550 - $10,432), from $5,535 to $15,653. The increase charged to expense has significantly exceeded write-offs.

As mentioned above, this increase may be due to customers' weakening credit quality. It may also be the case that INTU is overly conservative and is intentionally depressing its current profit. An inflated allowance can be used to absorb future receivable write-offs with no impact on future profit, or can be reversed in a future year to provide an immediate reduction in expense and consequent increase in profit. Either way, if the allowance account is inflated, the effect is to shift profit from the current period into the future.

P6-42 (15 minutes)

a. Average useful life = Cost / Depreciation expense
= ($12,760,421 - $370,949 - $920,599) / $868,808
= <u>13.2 years</u>

(Note: We eliminate land and construction in progress from the computation because land is never depreciated and construction in progress represents assets that are not in service yet and are consequently not depreciated).

The footnote indicates that buildings have estimated useful lives ranging from 10-50 years (27-year average) and Equipment from 3-20 years (11-year average).

b. Percent used up = Accumulated depreciation / Asset cost
= $6,757,280 / ($12,760,421 - $370,949 - $920,599)
= <u>58.9%</u>

(Note: We eliminate land and construction in progress from the computation because land is never depreciated and construction in progress represents assets that are not in service yet and are consequently not depreciated).

Assuming that assets are replaced evenly as they are used up, we would expect assets to be 50% depreciated, on average. Abbott Labs 58.9% is slightly higher than this level, but not high enough to cause concern that it will need significantly higher capital expenditures in the near future to replace aging assets.

C6-44 (30 minutes)

Reducing operating assets is an important means of increasing RNOA. Most companies focus first on reducing receivables and inventories. This is the low-hanging fruit that can lead to quick results. Some possible actions include the following:

a. Reducing receivables through:
   1. Better underwriting of credit quality
   2. Better controls to identify delinquencies, automated dunning notices, better collection procedures
   3. Increased attention to accuracy in invoicing

b. Reducing inventories through:
   1. Use of less costly components (of equal quality) and production with lower wage rates
   2. Elimination of product features not valued by customers
   3. Outsourcing to reduce product cost
   4. Just-in-time deliveries of raw materials
   5. Elimination of manufacturing bottlenecks to reduce work-in-process inventories
   6. Producing to order rather than to estimated demand to reduce finished goods inventories

c. Reducing PPE assets is much more difficult. The benefits, however, can be substantial. Some suggestions are the following:
   1. Sale of unused and unnecessary assets
   2. Acquisition of production and administrative assets in partnership with other companies for greater throughput
   3. Acquisition of finished or semifinished goods from suppliers to reduce manufacturing assets

Module 7

Reporting and Analyzing Intercorporate Investments

QUESTIONS

Q7-2. An *unrealized holding gain (loss)* is an increase (decrease) in the fair market value of an investment security that is still owned.

Q7-4. Significant influence gives the owner of the stock the ability to significantly influence the operating and financing activities of the company whose stock is owned. Normally, a 20% through 50% ownership of the company's voting stock provides evidence of significant influence.

The *equity method* is used to account for investments with significant influence. Such an investment is initially recorded at cost; the investment is increased by the proportionate share of the investee company's net income, and equity income is reported in the income statement. The investment account is decreased by dividends received on the investment, and is reported in the balance sheet at its book value. Unrealized appreciation in the market value of the investment is not recognized in the financial statements.

Q7-6. A stock investment representing more than 50% of the investee company's voting stock is generally viewed as conferring "control" over the investee company. The investor and investee companies must be consolidated for financial reporting purposes.

Q7-8. The $750,000 investment in Murray Company appearing in Finn Company's balance sheet, the $300,000 common stock and the $450,000 retained earnings appearing on Murray Company's balance sheet are all eliminated. The two balance sheets (less the accounts eliminated) are then summed to yield the consolidated balance sheet.

Q7-10. Limitations of consolidated statements include the possibility that consolidation "masks" the performances of poor companies. Likewise, rates of return, other ratios, and percentages calculated from consolidated statements might prove deceptive because they are composites. Consolidated statements also eliminate detail about product lines, divisional operations, and the relative profitability of various business segments. (Some of this information may be available in the footnote disclosures relating to the business segments of certain public firms, but these disclosures are limited in scope.) Finally, shareholders and creditors of subsidiary companies find it difficult to isolate amounts related to their legal rights by inspecting only consolidated statements.

M7-12 (15 minutes)

a. If the investment is accounted for as available-for-sale, Wasley will report the dividends received of $6,600 (6,000 shares × $1.10 per share) as income. The increase in the market price of the stock will not be recognized as income until the stock is sold. The unrealized gain of $6,000 is included in Accumulated Other Comprehensive Income in the stockholders' equity section of the balance sheet.

b. If the investment is accounted for as trading, Wasley will report $12,600 as income: $6,600 of dividend income plus $6,000 of income relating to the increase in the stock's market price [$13 – ($12 x 6,000 shares)].

M7-14 (20 minutes)

a. Given the 30% ownership, "significant influence" is presumed and the investment must be accounted for using the equity method. The year-end balance of the investment account is computed as follows:

Beginning balance	$1,000,000	
% Lang income earned	30,000	($100,000 × 0.3)
% Dividends received	(12,000)	($40,000 × 0.3)
Ending balance...	$1,018,000	

b. Stober reports income from investments of $30,000 ($100,000 × 0.3). Equity-method earnings are computed as the reported net income of the investee (Lang Company) multiplied by the percentage of the outstanding common stock owned by the investor (30%).

c. (1) In contrast to the market method, the equity method of accounting does not report investments at market value. Neither the balance sheet nor the income statement reflects the unrealized gain of $200,000.

M7-16 (15 minutes)

a. Merck reports its equity method investments at $3 billion on its 2005 balance sheet. Equity method investments are reported at adjusted cost, not at current market value. Adjusted cost is the original purchase price plus (minus) Merck's proportionate share of investee companies' profits (losses), less dividends received.

b. Merck accounts for dividends received on equity method investments as a reduction of the investment balance, not as income.

M7-18 (10 minutes)

Benartzi Company net income	$600,000
90% of $150,000 Liang Company net income	135,000
Consolidated net income	$735,000

E7-20 (30 minutes)

Trading Securities

	Balance Sheet						Income Statement		
Transaction	Cash Asset	+ Noncash Assets	= Liabil-ities	+ Contrib. Capital	+ Earned Capital		Rev-enues	– Expen-ses	= Net Income
1. Purchased 6,000 common shares of Liu, Inc., for $12 per share	-72,000	+72,000 Investment	=						
2. Received a cash dividend of $1.10 per common share from Liu	+6,600		=		+6,600 Retained Earnings		+6,600 Dividend Income		= +6,600
3. Year-end market price of Liu common stock is $11.25 per share.		-4,500 Investment	=		-4,500 Retained Earnings			+4,500 – Unrealized loss	= –4,500
4. Sold all 6,000 common shares of Liu for $66,900	+66,900	-67,500 Investment	=		-600 Retained Earnings			+600 – Loss on sale	= –600

Margin notes:

MS 72,000
　Cash 72,000

MS
72,000 |

Cash
　| 72,000

Cash 6,600
　DI 6,600

Cash
6,600 |

DI
　| 6,600

UL 4,500
　MS 4,500

UL
4,500 |

MS
　| 4,500

Cash 66,900
LS 600
　MS 67,500

Cash
66,900 |

LS
600

MS
　| 67,500

E7-20—continued.

Available-for-Sale Securities

Left-margin T-accounts:

```
        72,000
Cash    72,000

      MS
72,000|

     Cash
       | 72,000

sh   6,600
DI      6,600

    Cash
6,600|

     DI
       | 6,600

CI   4,500
MS      4,500

    AOCI
4,500|

     MS
       | 4,500

sh  66.900
     5,100
AOCI  4,500
MS   67,500

    Cash
66,900|

     LS
5,100|

    AOCI
       | 4,500

     MS
       | 67,500
```

Transaction	Balance Sheet					Income Statement		
	Cash Asset	+ Noncash Assets	= Liabil-ities	+ Contrib. Capital	+ Earned Capital	Rev-enues	– Expen-ses	= Net Income
1. Purchased 6,000 common shares of Liu, Inc., for $12 per share	-72,000	+72,000 Investment	=					
2. Received a cash dividend of $1.10 per common share from Liu	+6,600		=		+6,600 Retained Earnings	+6,600 Dividend Income		= +6,600
3. Year-end market price of Liu common stock is $11.25 per share.		-4,500 Investment	=		-4,500 AOCI			
4. Sold all 6,000 common shares of Liu for $66,900	+66,900	-67,500 Investment	=		+4,500 AOCI -5,100 Retained Earnings		– +5,100 Loss on sale	= -5,100

E7-22 (15 minutes)

a. Berkshire Hathaway's 2005 balance sheet reports the equity securities investment portfolio at the current market value of $46,721 million. Its unrealized gains of $25,382 million are concentrated in its holdings of American Express, Coca-Cola, and Wells Fargo.

b. Since unrealized gains on investments are reported in Accumulated Other Comprehensive Income (AOCI), rather than in its current income, we know that the investment portfolio is accounted for as an available-for-sale portfolio.

c. The $2,081 million is the change in the net unrealized gain from 2004 to 2005. This number is pretax. Berkshire Hathaway also discloses that it expects to pay taxes of $728 million on those gains if and when they are realized.

Note: The reclassification adjustment of $(6,261) million represents unrealized gains on investments that were included in AOCI at the beginning of the year and were realized in 2005 because the related investments were sold during the year. Because these gains are now recognized in current income (and retained earnings), they need to be removed from AOCI to avoid double-counting the gain in stockholders' equity (that is, in both AOCI and retained earnings).

E7-24 (20 minutes)

	Balance Sheet					Income Statement		
Transaction	Cash Asset	+ Noncash Assets	= Liabil- ities	+ Contrib. Capital	+ Earned Capital	Rev- enues	− Expen- ses	= Net Income
a. Purchased 12,000 common shares of Barth Co. at $9 per share; the shares represent 30% ownership in Barth	-108,000	+108,000 Investment =						
b. Received a cash dividend of $1.25 per common share from Barth	+15,000	-15,000 Investment =						
c. Recorded income from Barth stock investment when Barth's net income is $80,000		+24,000 Investment =			+24,000 Retained Earnings	+24,000 Equity Income		+24,000
d. Sold all 12,000 common shares of Barth for $120,500	+120,500	-117,000 Investment =			+3,500 Retained Earnings	+3,500 Gain on Sale		+3,500

Marginal notes (left side):

```
         108,000
Cash     108,000

EMI
08,000|

Cash
         | 108,000

sh       15,000
EMI          15,000

Cash
15,000|

EMI
         | 15,000

         24,000
EI           24,000

EMI
24,000|

EI
         | 24,000

sh       120,500
I            117,000
GN           3,500

Cash
20,500|

EMI
         | 117,000

GN
         | 3,500
```

E7-26 (30 minutes)

a. Market method accounting—Available-for-sale securities

	Transaction	Cash Asset	+	Noncash Assets	=	Liabil-ities	+	Contrib. Capital	+	Earned Capital	Rev-enues	−	Expen-ses	=	Net Income
MS 150,000 　Cash 150,000 **MS** 150,000 | **Cash** 　| 150,000	1. Ball purchased 10,000 common shares of Leftwich at $15 per share; which is a 15% ownership in Leftwich	−150,000 Cash		+150,000 Investment	=										
	2. Leftwich reported annual net income of $80,000	NO ENTRY													
Cash 11,000 　DI 11,000 **Cash** 11,000 | **DI** 　| 11,000	3. Received a cash dividend of $1.10 per common share from Leftwich	+11,000 Cash			=						+11,000 Retained Earnings	+11,000 Dividend Income			=	+11,000
MS 40,000 　AOCI 40,000 **MS** 40,000 | **AOCI** 　| 40,000	4. Year-end market price of Leftwich common stock is $19 per share			+40,000 Investment	=						+40,000 AOCI					

E7-26 (concluded)

b. Equity method accounting

Left-margin T-accounts:

```
    150,000
Cash    150,000

      EMI
60,000|

     Cash
      | 150,000

    24,000
EI      24,000

      EMI
24,000|

      EI
      | 24,000

Cash  11,000
EMI       11,000

     Cash
11,000|

      EMI
      | 11,000
```

Transaction	Balance Sheet					Income Statement		
	Cash Asset	+ Noncash Assets	= Liabil-ities	+ Contrib. Capital	+ Earned Capital	Rev-enues	– Expen-ses	= Net Income
1. Ball purchased 10,000 common shares of Leftwich at $15 per share; which is a 30% ownership in Leftwich	-150,000 Cash	+150,000 Investment	=					
2. Leftwich reported annual net income of $80,000		+24,000 Investment	=		+24,000 Retained Earnings	+24,000 Equity Income		= +24,000
3. Received a cash dividend of $1.10 per common share from Leftwich	+11,000 Cash	-11,000 Investment						
4. Year-end market price of Leftwich common stock is $19 per share	NO ENTRY							

E7-28 (25 minutes)

a. CAT reports these equity method investments on its balance sheet at $540 million. Since CAT reports an asset of only $540 million, most of the assets and all of the liabilities of the investee company are *not* reported on CAT's balance sheet. If this investment is critical to CAT's strategic plan, it, arguably, does not present a clear picture of the capital investment required to conduct CAT's business or the degree of financial leverage inherent in its operations, even though its accounting is in conformity with GAAP.

b. Although CAT is not directly obligated for the debts of these unconsolidated affiliates (unless it has legally guaranteed those debts), if the affiliates were to fail, would CAT have to invest additional capital to support it? Probably not, from a strictly legal standpoint. Yet, if this investment is necessary for CAT's strategic plan, it might find it difficult to arrange future ventures of this type if it does not support the failing investee. This means that there can be an *effective* liability even when no *legal* liability exists. Analysts can, of course, replace the equity investment with the assets and liabilities to which it relates (pro forma consolidation for analysis purposes) if they feel consolidated numbers better represent the company's balance sheet and income statement.

c. The equity method reports only CAT's proportion of the affiliated companies' equity as an investment on the balance sheet and CAT's proportion of the affiliated companies' earnings on the income statement. As a result, the equity method, arguably, omits assets and liabilities from the face of CAT's balance sheet and sales and expenses from the income statement (compared with the assets and liabilities and sales and expenses that would be recorded with consolidation). Net income and stockholders' equity are the same whether the equity method or consolidation is used. Thus, ROE is the same, but net operating profit margins (net operating income after tax / sales) and net operating asset turnover rates (sales / average net operating assets) will differ with the omission of assets and sales.

E7-30 (30 minutes)

a. AT&T's investment in and advances to Cingular reported on AT&T's balance sheet at December, 2005 total $31,404. AT&T's advances to Cingular at 2005 are $4,108 at December, 2005. The interest earned on these advances is $311. The equity investment is, therefore, $26,985 ($31,404 - $4,108 - $311).

Cingular's equity at 2005 is $6,049 million + $73,270 million - $10,008 million - $24,333 million = $44,978 million. The equity investment, thus, represents its 60% ($26,985 million / $44,978 million) equity interest.

b. Cingular paid no dividends during 2005. The receipt of dividends reduces the equity method investment on AT&T's books. The reconciliation of the investment balance from 2004 to 2005 shows no reduction due to the payment of dividends.

c. AT&T reports equity income equal to its proportionate share of Cingular's net income or $200 million (60% × $333 million).

d. Undistributed earnings are earnings that have not yet been paid out as dividends. This is retained earnings. Of Cingular's $44,978 million of stockholders' equity, $2,711 is, apparently, retained earnings.

e. The equity method reports only the equity owned as an investment on the balance sheet and equity in earnings on the income statement. As a result, use of this method, arguably, omits assets and liabilities from the face of the balance sheet and sales and expenses from the income statement (compared with the assets and liabilities and sales and expenses that would be recorded with consolidation). Net income and stockholders' equity are the same whether the equity method or consolidation is used. Thus, ROE is the same. But net operating profit margins (net operating income after tax / sales) and net operating asset turnover rates (sales / average net operating assets) will differ with the omission of assets and sales.

f. The equity method of accounting for investments must be used if the investor company can exert "significant influence," but cannot "control" the investee company. AT&T discloses in its footnote that it shares control equally with the other joint venture partner (equal voting rights and representation on the board of directors). Since AT&T does not "control" Cingular, the investment does not need to be consolidated.

g. Following the merger with Bell South, AT&T will own 100% of Cingular and, therefore, will control that company. Cingular must then be consolidated with its parent, rather than accounted for as an equity method investment.

E7-32 (30 minutes)

	Rayburn	Kanodia	Consolidating adjustments	Consolidated
Investment in Kanodia.	$ 600,000		(600,000)	$ 0
Other assets	2,300,000	$700,000	20,000	3,020,000
Goodwill.........................			40,000	40,000
Total assets	$2,900,000	$700,000		$3,060,000
Liabilities.......................	$ 900,000	$160,000		$1,060,000
Contributed Capital	1,400,000	300,000	(300,000)	1,400,000
Retained earnings	600,000	240,000	(240,000)	600,000
Total liabilities & stockholders' equity.....	$2,900,000	$700,000		$3,060,000

E7-34 (20 minutes)

a. The investment is initially recorded on Engel's balance sheet at the purchase price of $16.8 million, including $600,000 of goodwill. Since the market value of Ball is less than the carrying amount of the investment on Engel's balance sheet, the goodwill might be impaired. To determine impairment, the imputed value of the goodwill is determined to be $12.5 million - $12.3 million = $200,000. Since this is less than the carrying amount, the goodwill is impaired.

b. Goodwill must be written down by $400,000. The write-down will reduce the carrying amount of goodwill by $400,000 and yield a loss in Engel's income statement, thus reducing retained earnings by that amount.

E7-36^B (60 minutes)

a.

Cash paid...	$210,000
Fair market value of shares issued............................	180,000
Purchase price	390,000
Less: Book value of Harris......................................	280,000
Excess payment..	110,000
Excess payment assigned to specific accounts based on fair market value:	
—Buildings...	40,000
—Patent	30,000
—Goodwill	40,000
Total excess payment..	$110,000

b.

Accounts	Easton, Inc.	Harris Co.	Consolidation Entries		Consolidated Totals
Cash	$ 84,000	$ 40,000			$ 124,000
Receivables	160,000	90,000			250,000
Inventory	220,000	130,000			350,000
Investment in Harris	390,000		[S] [A]	(280,000) (110,000)	-
Land	100,000	60,000			160,000
Buildings, net	400,000	110,000	[A]	40,000	550,000
Equipment, net	120,000	50,000			170,000
Patent	-	-	[A]	30,000	30,000
Goodwill	-	-	[A]	40,000	40,000
Totals	$1,474,000	$ 480,000			$1,674,000
Balances					
Accounts payable	$ 160,000	$ 30,000			$ 190,000
Long-term liabilities	380,000	170,000			550,000
Common stock	500,000	40,000	[S]	(40,000)	500,000
Additional paid-in capital	74,000	-			74,000
Retained earnings	360,000	240,000	[S]	(240,000)	360,000
Totals	$1,474,000	$ 480,000			$1,674,000

E7-36—continued

c. The fair-market-value adjustment to fixed assets will be depreciated over the assets' estimated useful lives. The patent will be amortized over its useful life. Finally, intangible assets with an indeterminate useful life (such as goodwill) are not amortized, but are tested annually for impairment, or more often if circumstances require.

PROBLEMS

P7-38 (50 minutes)

a. Available-for-sale investments are reported at market value on the balance sheet. Thus, MetLife's bond investments are reported at:

   $230,050 million as of 2005
   $176,377 million as of 2004

b. Net unrealized gains for 2005 are
   $6,124 million ($8,329 million - $2,205 million)
   Net unrealized gains for 2004 are
   $9,766 million ($10,267 million - $501 million)

   Since the investments are accounted for as available-for-sale, the net unrealized gains did not affect reported income for 2005 and 2004. (Note: Had these investments been accounted for as trading securities, those unrealized gains and losses would have affected reported income.)

c. Realized gains (losses) are gains (losses) that occur as a result of sales of securities. These are reported in the income statement and affect reported income.

   Unrealized gains (losses) reflect the difference between the current market price of the security and its acquisition cost. Only unrealized gains (losses) from trading securities are reported in income.

d. Net unrealized gains (losses) for 2005 are $6,124 million ($8,329 million - $2,205 million). The amounts reported in the investment footnote are pretax, and the amount reported in the Accumulated Other Comprehensive Income (AOCI) section of stockholders' equity on MetLife's balance sheet is after-tax. This means that MetLife reports approximately $2.1 billion of deferred taxes relating to these 2005 net unrealized gains.

P7-40 (60 minutes)

a. Yes, each individual company (parent and subsidiary) maintains its own financial statements. This is necessary to report on the activities of the individual units and to report to the respective stakeholders of each unit, including tax authorities.

   The purpose of consolidation is to combine these separate financial statements to more clearly reflect the operations and financial condition of the combined (whole) entity.

b. The Investment in Financial Products Subsidiaries is reported on the parent's (Machinery and Engine's) balance sheet at <u>$3,253 million</u>. This is the same balance as reported for stockholders' equity of the Financial Products subsidiary. This relation will always exist so long as the investment is originally purchased at book value.

c. The consolidated balance sheet more clearly reflects the actual assets and liabilities of the combined company compared to the equity method of accounting. That is, the consolidated balance sheet better reflects operations of the entire entity as far as investors and creditors are concerned.

   The equity method of accounting that is used by the parent company to account for its investment in the subsidiary reflects only its proportionate share (100% in this case) of the investee company's stockholders' equity and does not report the individual assets and liabilities comprising that equity.

d. The consolidating adjustments generally accomplish three objectives:
   (i) They eliminate the equity method investment on the parent's balance sheet and replace it with the subsidiary's actual assets and liabilities.

   (ii) They record any additional assets that are included in the investment balance that may not be reflected on the subsidiary's balance sheet, like goodwill, for example.

   (iii) They eliminate any intercompany sales and receivables / payables.

e. The consolidated stockholders' equity and the stockholders' equity of the parent company are equal. This equality will always be the case. The consolidation process replaces the investment account with the individual assets and liabilities to which it relates. Thus, stockholders' equity remains unaffected.

f. Consolidated net income will equal the net income of the parent company. The reason for this is that the parent reflects the income of the subsidiary via the equity method of accounting for its investment.

The consolidation process merely replaces the equity income account with the individual sales and expenses to which it relates. Net income is unaffected.

g. The consolidated balance sheet is not affected by market-value changes in the subsidiary's stock. Unrealized gains on the stock of a subsidiary are not reflected on the consolidated balance sheet or on the income statement. Instead, the subsidiary is reflected on the balance sheet at its purchase price, net of depreciation and amortization, just like any other asset. The consolidation process merely replaces the investment account with the actual assets and liabilities to which it relates. Thus, substantial unrealized gains subsequent to the acquisition are not reflected in the consolidated financial statements.

CASES

C7-42 (30 minutes)

General Electric Company provides a comprehensive listing of the components of its corporate governance policy, and serves as an appropriate example. The headings are as follows (complete descriptions can be found at: www.ge.com/en/citizenship/governance/govprinc.htm

1. Role of Board and Management.
2. Functions of Board
3. Qualifications
4. Independence of Directors
5. Size of Board and Selection Process
6. Board Committees
7. Independence of Committee Members
8. Meetings of Non-Employee Directors
9. Self-Evaluation
10. Setting Board Agenda
11. Ethics and Conflicts of Interest
12. Reporting of Concerns to Non-Employee Directors or Audit Committee
13. Compensation of the Board
14. Succession Plan
15. Annual Compensation Review of Senior Management
16. Access to Senior Management
17. Access to Independent Advisors
18. Director Education
19. Policy on Poison Pills
20. Majority Vote Policy
21. Stock Ownership Requirement

Module 8

Reporting and Analyzing Nonowner Financing

QUESTIONS

Q8-2. An accrual is the recognition of an event in the financial statements even though no external transaction has occurred. Accruals can involve both liabilities (and expenses) and assets (and revenues).

Accruals are vital to the fair presentation of the financial condition of a company as they impact both the recognition of revenue and the matching of expenses.

Q8-4. Bonds are reported at historical cost, that is, the face amount plus (minus) unamortized premium (discount). The market price of the bonds varies inversely with the prevailing interest rates, which fluctuate continuously. Differences between the market price of a bond and its carrying amount (net book value) represent unrealized gains and losses. These unrealized gains (losses) are not reflected in the financial statements (although they are disclosed in the footnotes). They must be recognized if the issuer repurchases the bonds because at that point the gains or losses become "realized."

Gains and losses from bond redemptions are not real economic gains and losses. The recognition of the gain (loss) on redemption results from the use of historical costing for bonds. The gain (loss) that is reported upon redemption will be offset by correspondingly lower (higher) interest payments in the future. The financial statements recognize neither the present value of these future interest payments, nor the present value of the difference between the current face amount of the bond and the former face amount. These present values exactly offset the reported gain (loss); thus, no "real" gain (loss) has been realized.

Q8-6. Companies report gains or losses on bond redemption because they use historical cost accounting. The redemption gain or loss is offset by the present value of lower (higher) interest payments in the future. The present value of those future interest payments, as well as the present value of the difference between the current face amount of the bond and the former face amount, are not recognized in the financial statements, and no "real" economic gain or loss occurs. For analysis purposes, gains or losses on bond redemption are usually considered transitory items.

MINI EXERCISES

M 8-8 (10 minutes)

Transaction	Balance Sheet					Income Statement		
	Cash Asset	+ Noncash Assets	= Liabil- ities	+ Contrib. Capital	+ Earned Capital	Rev- enues	– Expen- ses	= Net Income
To accrue interest at December 31*			= +24 Interest Payable		-24 Retained Earnings		+24 – Interest Expense	= -24

IE   24
IP   24

IE
24 |

IP
| 24

* $7,200 \times 0.08 \times 15/365$

M8-10 (10 minutes)

a. Boston Scientific is offering bonds with a coupon (stated) rate of 4.25% when the market rate (yield) is higher at 4.349%. To obtain this expected rate of return, the bonds must sell at a discount price of 99.476 (99.476% of par).

b. The first bond matures in 2011 while the second matures in 2017. The market demands a higher rate (yield) for a longer maturity debt instrument.

M8-12 (10 minutes)

a. The $1.4 billion indicates that BMY has bonds maturing in 2008 that will require payment of $1.4 billion. BMY will either pay these off with operating cash flows in 2008 or will issue more debt.

b. We assume that BMY will need to pay off the bonds when they mature. This will result in cash outflows that must come from operating activities if the bonds cannot be refinanced prior to their maturity. The size of these payments could affect BMY's liquidity and or solvency in 2008 and we need to carefully assess the company's ability to repay the debt given current levels of cash flow and existing debt.

M8-14 (15 minutes)

a. Financial ratios used in bond covenants are typically designed to protect the bondholders against detrimental managerial actions. Restrictions might prohibit the impairment of liquidity, the increasing of financial leverage, and the paying of cash dividends. In addition, bondholders usually impose various covenants prohibiting the acquisition of other companies or the divestiture of business segments without bondholders' consent. All of these covenants, by design, restrict management in actions that might increase the bondholders' risk.

b. Managers who face imminent default in one or more bond covenants, would likely take action to avoid such default. These actions can include, for example, operational responses, such as reducing R&D or advertising to improve profitability, or leaning on the trade (by delaying payment), reducing receivables (via early payment incentives), or reducing inventory (by marketing promotions or delaying restocking) to boost cash balances. Actions can also include fraudulent or aggressive accounting tactics, such as improper recognition of revenues or delayed recognition of expenses.

M8-16 (15 minutes)

	Balance Sheet					Income Statement		
Transaction	Cash Asset	+ Noncash Assets	= Liabilities	+ Contrib. Capital	+ Earned Capital	Revenues	− Expenses	= Net Income
To retire bonds at 101, remove unamortized discount and report loss on bond retirement*	-252.5 Cash		-250 Long-Term Debt +7 Discount on Bonds		-9.5 Retained Earnings		+9.5 Loss on Bond Retirement	-9.5

Side notations:

243
9.5
sh 252.5

LTD
243

LS
9.5

Cash
253

* Retirement price = \$252,500 = \$250,000 × 101%
Original discount = (100% − 96%) × \$250,000 = \$10,000
Unamortized discount = \$10,000 - \$3,000 = \$7,000

M8-18 (10 minutes)

a. Financial leverage (which measures debt levels) is one of the ratios that bond rating agencies use to determine credit ratings. Generally, the higher (lower) the financial leverage, the lower (higher) the bond rating. Therefore, by reducing its debt level, GM will reduce leverage and improve its bond rating.

b. Higher credit ratings on bond issues result in a lower yield expected by bond purchasers and higher bond issuance proceeds realized by the company. This will lower GM's borrowing costs.

M8-20 (15 minutes)

a. Selling price of zero coupon bonds discounted at 8%

Present value of principal repayment ($500,000 × 0.45639[a]) $228,195

[a]Table 1, 20 periods at 4%

b. Selling price of zero coupon bonds discounted at 10%

Present value of principal repayment ($500,000 × 0.37689[a]) $188,445

[a]Table 1, 20 periods at 5%

M8-22 (30 minutes)

a.

Data Inputs into Excel -- PRICE(settlement,maturity,rate,yld,redemption,frequency,basis)	
1/1/2007	Settlement date
1/1/2017	Maturity date
9.00%	Percent semiannual coupon
8.00%	Percent yield
$100	Redemption value
2	Frequency is semiannual (see above)
1	actual/actual basis

	Percent of Par	Sale Proceeds
Price.........	106.7951632	$533,975.82
		($500,000 × 1.067951632)

b.

Period	Interest	Cash Paid	Premium Amortization	Premium Balance	Carrying Amount
0				33,975.82	533,975.82
1	21,359.03	22,500.00	1,140.97	32,834.85	532,834.85
2	21,313.39	22,500.00	1,186.61	31,648.24	531,648.24
3	21,265.93	22,500.00	1,234.07	30,414.17	530,414.17
4	21,216.57	22,500.00	1,283.43	29,130.74	529,130.74
5	21,165.23	22,500.00	1,334.77	27,795.97	527,795.97
6	21,111.84	22,500.00	1,388.16	26,407.81	526,407.81
7	21,056.31	22,500.00	1,443.69	24,964.12	524,964.12
8	20,998.56	22,500.00	1,501.44	23,462.68	523,462.68
9	20,938.51	22,500.00	1,561.49	21,901.19	521,901.19
10	20,876.05	22,500.00	1,623.95	20,277.24	520,277.24
11	20,811.09	22,500.00	1,688.91	18,588.33	518,588.33
12	20,743.53	22,500.00	1,756.47	16,831.86	516,831.86
13	20,673.27	22,500.00	1,826.73	15,005.14	515,005.14
14	20,600.21	22,500.00	1,899.79	13,105.34	513,105.34
15	20,524.21	22,500.00	1,975.79	11,129.56	511,129.56
16	20,445.18	22,500.00	2,054.82	9,074.74	509,074.74
17	20,362.99	22,500.00	2,137.01	6,937.73	506,937.73
18	20,277.51	22,500.00	2,222.49	4,715.24	504,715.24
19	20,188.61	22,500.00	2,311.39	2,403.85	502,403.85
20	20,096.15	22,500.00	2,403.85	0.00	500,000.00

©Cambridge Business Publishers, 2008

EXERCISES

E8-24 (20 minutes)

1. Neither record nor disclose (the loss is not probable).

2. Record a current liability for the note. At the financial statement date, record a liability for any interest that has been incurred since the note was signed.

3. Disclose in a footnote (the loss is reasonably possible but the amount cannot be estimated).

4. Record warranty liability on balance sheet and recognize expense in income statement (costs are probable and reasonably estimable).

E8-26 (15 minutes)

Demski company must accrue the $25,000 of wages that have been earned even though these wages will not be paid until the first of next month. The accrual will:

- increase wages payable by $25,000 on the balance sheet (current liability)

- increase wages expense by $25,000 in the income statement (operating expense)

Failure to make this accrual (called an adjusting entry) would understate liabilities, understate wages expense, overstate income, and overstate stockholders' equity.

E8-28 (25 minutes)

	Balance Sheet						Income Statement		
Transaction	Cash Asset	+ Noncash Assets	= Liabil- ities	+ Contrib. Capital	+ Earned Capital		Rev- enues	− Expen- ses	= Net Income
1. Issue $700,000, mortgage note payable	+700,000 Cash		+700,000 = Long-Term Debt						
2. Make first installment on June 30th (i)	−50,854 Cash		−8,854 = Long-Term Debt		−42,000 Retained Earnings			+42,000 − Interest Expense	= −42,000
3. Make second installment on December 31st (ii)	−50,854 Cash		−9,385 = Long-Term Debt		−41,469 Retained Earnings			+41,469 − Interest Expense	= −41,469

Left-margin T-accounts:

```
 h 700,000       Cash            LTD
TD 700,000     0,000 |              | 700,000

  42,000          IE             LTD           Cash
D  8,854      2,000 |         8,854 |              | 50,854
ash 50,854

  41,469          IE             LTD           Cash
TD 9,385     41,469 |         9,385 |              | 50,854
Cash 50,854
```

i 0.06 × $700,000 = $42,000 interest expense. The difference between interest expense and the cash payment is the reduction of the principal amount of the loan ($50,854 − $42,000 = $8,854).

ii 0.06 × ($700,000 - $8,854) = $41,469 interest expense. The difference between interest expense and the cash payment is the reduction of the principal amount of the loan ($50,854 − $41,469 = $9,385).

E8-30 (25 minutes)

Cash 500,000
   LTD   500,000

	Balance Sheet						Income Statement			
Transaction	Cash Asset	+ Noncash Assets	= Liabil-ities	+ Contrib. Capital	+ Earned Capital		Rev-enues	− Expen-ses	= Net Income
1. Issue bonds May 1, 2007	+500,000 Cash		= +500,000 Long Term Debt						
2. Pay interest on October 31, 2007 [1]	−22,500 Cash		=		−22,500 Retained Earnings			− +22,500 Interest Expense	= −22,500
3. Retire $300,000 of bonds at 101 [2]	−303,000 Cash		= −300,000 Long-Term Debt					− +3,000 Loss	= −3,000

T-accounts (left margin):

Cash | 500,000
LTD | 500,000

IE 22,500
  Cash 22,500

IE | 22,500
Cash | 22,500

LTD 300,000
LS   3,000
  Cash 303,000

LTD | 300,000
LS | 3,000
LTD | 303,000

[1] $500{,}000 \times 0.09 \times 1/2 = \$22{,}500$ interest expense. Since the bonds were sold at par, there is no discount or premium amortization.

[2] Cash required to retire $300,000 of bonds at 101 = $300{,}000 \times 1.01 = \$303{,}000$. The difference between the cash paid and the carrying amount of the bonds is the loss on the redemption. In this case, the loss is $3,000.

E8-32 (25 minutes)

a. Selling price of bonds

Present value of principal repayment ($800,000 × 0.20829)............$166,632
Present value of interest payments ($36,000 × 19.79277) 712,540
Selling price of bonds...$879,172

b.

Transaction	Balance Sheet						Income Statement		
	Cash Asset	+ Noncash Assets	= Liabil- ities	+ Contrib. Capital	+ Earned Capital		Rev- enues	− Expen- ses	= Net Income
1. Issue $800,000, 9% bonds to yield 8%(1)	+879,172 Cash		+879,172 = Long-Term Debt						
2. Pay interest on June 30th (2)	−36,000 Cash		−833 = Long-Term Debt		−35,167 Retained Earnings			+35,167 Interest Expense	= −35,167
3. Pay interest on December 31st (3)	−36,000 Cash		−866 = Long-Term Debt		−35,134 Retained Earnings			+35,134 Interest Expense	= −35,134

(Left margin T-account entries:)

Cash 879,172
LTD 879,172

Cash
879,172 |

LTD
| 879,172
35,167
LTD 833
Cash 36,000

IE
35,167 |

LTD
833 |

Cash
| 36,000
35,134
LTD 866
Cash 36,000

IE
35,134 |

LTD
866 |

Cash
| 36,000

---

[1] The bond is reported at its sale price, which represents the par value of $800,000 plus the premium of $79,172.

[2] The cash paid = bond face amount × coupon rate ($800,000 × 0.045 = $36,000). The interest expense = bond carrying amount × discount rate ($879,172 × 0.04 = $35,167). The difference between the two is the amortization of the premium, which decreases the carrying amount of the bond.

[3] The cash paid =bond face amount × coupon rate ($800,000 × 0.045 = $36,000). The interest expense = bond carrying amount × discount rate [($879,171 - $833) × 0.04 = $35,134]. The difference between the two is the amortization of the premium, which decreases the carrying amount of the bond.

E8-34^A (30 minutes)

a. 1. $90,000 × 0.46319 = $41,687
   2. $90,000 × 0.45639 = $41,075

b. $1,000 × 5.33493   = $5,335

c. $600 × 17.29203   = $10,375

d. $500,000 × 0.38554 = $192,770

E8-36 (25 minutes)

a. Selling price of bonds

Present value of principal repayment ($400,000 × 0.61391)........	$245,564
Present value of interest payments ($26,000 × 7.72173)	200,765
Selling price of bonds..	$446,329

b.

	Balance Sheet						Income Statement		
Transaction	Cash Asset	+	Noncash Assets	=	Liabil- ities	+	Contrib. Capital	+	Earned Capital
	Rev- enues	−	Expen- ses	=	Net Income				

1. Issue $400,000, 13% bonds to yield 10%[(1)]	+446,329 Cash		= +446,329 Long-Term Debt
2. Pay interest on June 30th [(2)]	−26,000 Cash		= −3,684 Long-Term Debt
3. Pay interest on December 31st [(3)]	−26,000 Cash		= −3,868 Long-Term Debt

(Transaction 2): −22,316 Retained Earnings ... +22,316 Interest Expense = −22,316

(Transaction 3): −22,132 Retained Earnings ... +22,132 Interest Expense = −22,132

(T-account notations in left margin:)

Cash 446,329
LTD 446,329

Cash
446,329 |

LTD
| 446,329
22,316
LTD 3,684
Cash 26,000

IE
22,316 |

LTD
3,684 |

Cash
| 26,000
22,132
LTD 3,868
Cash 26,000

IE
22,132 |

LTD
3,868 |

Cash
| 26,000

---

[1] The bond is reported at its sale price, which represents the par value of $400,000 plus the premium of $46,329.

[2] The cash paid = bond face amount × coupon rate ($400,000 × 0.065 = $26,000). The interest expense = bond carrying amount × discount rate ($446,329 × 0.05 = $22,316). The difference between the two ($3,684) is the amortization of the premium, which decreases the carrying amount of the bond.

[3] The cash paid = bond face amount × coupon rate ($400,000 × 0.065 = $26,000). The interest expense = bond carrying amount × discount rate [($446,329 − $3,684) × 0.05 = $22,132]. The difference between the two ($3,868) is the amortization of the premium, which decreases the carrying amount of the bond.

PROBLEMS

P8-38 (20 minutes)

a. CVS paid $135.9 million for interest in 2005. Its average long-term debt during 2005, is $2,515.6 million [($2,189.1 million + $2,842.1 million) / 2]. Therefore, the average coupon rate is 5.4%, computed as $135.9 / $2,515.6.

CVS reports 2005 interest expense of $117.0 million on average long-term debt of $2,515.6 million [($2,189.1 million + $2,842.1 million) / 2] for an average effective (yield) rate of 4.65%.

b. CVS reports coupon rates ranging from 3.875% to 8.52% (the latter is on $114.0 million vs. $300 million for the lowest rate). Thus, the average coupon rate of 5.4% seems reasonable given the information disclosed in the long-term debt footnote. One might also weight the given interest rates by the total loan amounts to better estimate that rate.

c. Interest paid can differ from interest expense if the bonds are sold at a premium or at a discount. Interest expense is computed using the effective interest rate method, which uses the debt's net book value and the effective (yield) interest rate (the market rate prevailing when the bond was issued).

P8-40 (50 minutes)

a. Following is the graph of YTM vs. Maturity for Comcast long-term debt:

Yield to Maturity as a Funciton of Maturity

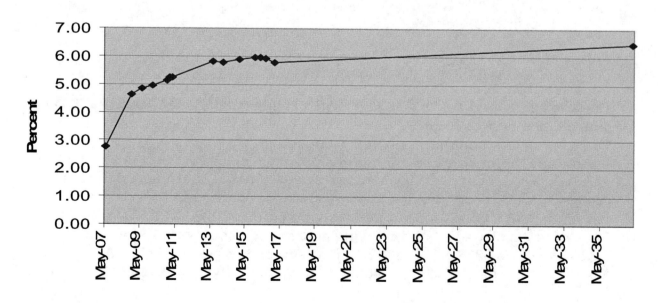

The graph shows an increasing yield as the maturity lengthens. This is generally the pattern we observe for market yields. The higher yields compensate investors for the collection risk and inflation risk they assume by tying up their cash in long-term issues.

b. The Comcast ratios relate to the following debt classifications using the table in Exhibit 8.6:

Ratio	Level	Implied Bond rating
EBIT interest coverage	2.05	BB
EBITDA interest coverage	4.73	BBB -- BB
FFO / Total debt	0.25	BBB -- BB
Free operating cash flow / Total debt	0.10	A -- BBB
Return on capital	0.02	B -- CCC
Operating income / Sales	16.6%	A -- BBB
Long-term debt / Capital	0.35	A -- BBB
Total debt / Capital	0.36	AAA -- AA

Comcast carries substantial levels of debt, but also has significant equity capital. From a capitalization standpoint, the company might warrant a higher credit rating, but the income-related ratios are solidly in the BBB range, which is the company's current rating on its bonds.

c. The market prices of the bonds are set to provide the yield that the market demands given the credit rating of the company (BBB) and the maturity of the bond. Whether the bonds trade above or below their coupon rates depends on the level of those coupon rates in the context of what the market demands for a return. Bonds with higher (lower) coupon rates will trade at higher (lower) prices.

CASES

C8-42 (15 minutes)

Failure to abide by bond covenants can result in serious consequences. Ensuring that the company has complied with such restrictions is an important area of corporate governance. Companies can utilize internal and external auditing to monitor compliance. The board of directors must also be aware of the possibility of earnings management in order to avoid default on bond covenants. As the possibility of default increases, so does management's desire to avoid default by whatever means it can, including the earnings management.

Module 9

Reporting and Analyzing Owner Financing

QUESTIONS

Q9-2. Typically, preferred stock has the following features: 1) Preferential claim to dividends and to assets in liquidation, 2) Cumulative dividend rights, and 3) No voting rights.

Q9-4. Dividends in arrears on preferred stock are the cumulative preferred dividends that have *not* been paid to date. The dividends in arrears and a current dividend must be paid to preferred stockholders before common stockholders can receive any dividends. In the example, the company must pay preferred stockholders $90,000 in dividends ($500,000 × 0.06 × 3 years = $90,000) before paying any dividends to common stockholders.

Q9-6. Contributed capital represents the total investment "contributed" by shareholders when they purchase stock. It is considered contributed because the company is under no legal obligation to repay the shareholders. Earned capital represents the cumulative net income that the company has earned, less the portion of that income that has been paid out to shareholders in the form of dividends.

When profit is earned, the company can either pay out a portion of that profit as a dividend or reinvest the earnings in order to grow the company. In fact, many companies title the Retained Earnings account as Reinvested Earnings. Earned capital, thus, represents an implicit investment by the shareholders in the form of foregone dividends.

Q9-8. A stock split refers to the issuance of additional shares to the current stockholders in proportion to their ownership interests. This is normally accompanied by a proportionate reduction in the par or stated value of the stock. For example, a 2-for-1 stock split doubles the number of shares outstanding and halves the par or stated value of the shares. The market value of the stock typically falls to half in the event of a 2:1 stock split. Consequently, there is no change to the company's balance sheet; the amount of contributed capital remains the same after the stock split. The major reason for a stock split is to reduce the share price of the stock. It is believed that when the stock price is very high, few investors can afford to purchase the stock. Another possible reason is to lead shareholders to believe that there has been some distribution of value.

Q9-10. The $2,400 increase should not be shown on the income statement as income or gain. The $2,400 is properly treated as additional paid-in capital and is shown as such in the stockholders' equity section of the balance sheet. The latter treatment is justified because treasury stock transactions are considered capital rather than operating transactions. GAAP does not permit corporations to "own" themselves. Thus, the company's treasury stock is not shown as an investment.

Q9-12. A stock dividend is the distribution of additional shares of a corporation's stock to its existing stockholders. A stock dividend does not change a stockholder's relative ownership interest, because each stockholder owns the same fractional share of the corporation before and after the stock dividend. There is empirical evidence, however, suggesting that the stock price does not decline fully to compensate for the additional shares issued. That is, if a company does a 2-for-1 stock split, the market price of each share should be half as much after the split. This does not always happen. The price usually falls to 52% to 55% of the pre split price. One hypothesis to explain this phenomenon is that, by splitting the stock, the company is sending a signal to the market that the firm is going to have a price increase (which warrants the split).

Q9-14. Many companies repurchase shares (as Treasury Stock) in order to offset the dilutive effects of stock options, because stock options increase the number of outstanding shares in the diluted EPS calculation. Stock repurchases typically decrease cash, which has immediate and ongoing economic effects. Some companies increase debt to repurchase stock. Analysts need to be concerned about the consequences of increased leverage solely to prop up diluted EPS.

Q9-16. Other Comprehensive Income (OCI) represents changes in stockholders' equity that are caused by factors other than net income and transactions with the company's shareholders. Some examples include unrealized gains (losses) on available-for-sale securities, foreign currency translation adjustments (current rate method only), unrealized gains (losses) on certain types of derivatives, and minimum and other pension liability adjustments.

Q9-18. When a convertible bond is converted, the company removes both the face amount and any associated unamortized premium or discount from the balance sheet. The stock is, then, issued for a "purchase price" equal to the bond's book value (face amount net of any unamortized premium or discount). This purchase price is, then, allocated to common stock and additional paid-in capital. No gain or loss is ever reported upon the conversion.

MINI EXERCISES

M9-20 (10 minutes)

		Balance Sheet						Income Statement		
	Transaction	Cash Asset	+ Noncash Assets	= Liabil-ities	+ Contrib. Capital	+ Earned Capital		Rev-enues	− Expen-ses	= Net Income
h 864,000 S 180,000 PIC 684,000										
Cash 4,000	Issue 18,000 shares of $10 par value preferred stock at $48 cash per share	+864,000 Cash		=	+180,000 Preferred Stock +684,000 Additional Paid-in Capital					
PS 180,000										
APIC 684,000										
h 4,440,000 S 240,000 PIC 4,200,000										
Cash 440,000	Issue 120,000 shares of $2 par value common stock at $37 cash per share	+4,440,000 Cash		=	+240,000 Common Stock +4,200,000 Additional Paid-in Capital					
CS 240,000										
APIC 4,200,000										

M9-22 (10 minutes)

Cash 1,250,000
PS 500,000
APIC 750,000

	Transaction	Cash Asset	+	Noncash Assets	=	Liabil- ities	+	Contrib. Capital	+	Earned Capital	Rev- enues	−	Expen- ses	=	Net Income
	Issue 5,000 shares of $100 par value preferred stock at $250 cash per share	+1,250,000 Cash			=			+500,000 Preferred Stock +750,000 Additional Paid-in Capital							
	Repurchase 5,000 shares of $1 par value common stock at $83 per share	−415,000 Cash			=					−415,000 Treasury Stock					

Left-side ledger entries:

Cash 1,250,000 |

PS | 500,000

APIC | 750,000

TS 415,000
Cash 415,000

TS 415,000 |

Cash | 415,000

M9-24 (15 minutes)

a. 103,300,000 shares issued × $0.01 par = $1,033,000. This amount is reported in thousands as $1,033.

b. Outstanding shares are equal to issued shares less repurchased shares. For 2006, Abercrombie & Fitch has 103,300,000 − 15,573,789 = 87,726,211 shares outstanding.

c. Total proceeds from the sale are the sum of the common stock and additional paid-in capital accounts. For 2006, this total is $162,711,000 ($1,033,000 + $161,678,000). The average price at which Abercrombie issued common stock is $1.58 ($162,711,000 / 103,300,000 shares).

d. The average price at which Abercrombie & Fitch repurchased treasury stock is $35.37 ($550,795,000 / 15,573,789 shares).

M9-26 (10 minutes)

		Balance Sheet					Income Statement		
Transaction	Cash Asset	+ Noncash Assets	= Liabil-ities	+ Contrib. Capital	+ Earned Capital	Rev-enues	− Expen-ses	= Net Income
Declare and pay stock dividend.		=		+14,000 Common Stock +44,800 Additional Paid-in Capital	−58,800 Retained Earnings		−	=

Left margin ledger:

```
         58,800
  S      14,000
PIC      44,800

    RE
58,800 |

    CS
       | 14,000

  APIC
       | 44,800
```

Stock dividend = $58,800: market price of the shares distributed (70,000 shares × 4% × $21).

M9-28 (15 minutes)

		Distribution to	
		Preferred	Common
a.	$1,000,000 × 6%...	$60,000	
	Balance to common...		$100,000
	Per share		
	$60,000 / 20,000 shares	$3.00	
	$100,000 / 80,000 shares		$1.25
b.	$1,000,000 × 6% × 2 years	$120,000	
	Balance to common...		$40,000
	Per share		
	$120,000 / 20,000 shares	$6.00	
	$40,000 / 80,000 shares		$0.50

M9-30 (10 minutes)

a. A spin-off is a distribution of shares of a subsidiary to the company's shareholders in the form of a dividend. A split-off is the exchange of shares between the company and its shareholders. In a split-off, Bristol Myers' shareholders would exchange their shares in the company for Zimmer shares owned by Bristol Myers. The end result of a spin-off and a split-off is the same economically (the shareholders end up owning the subsidiary directly rather than indirectly via the company), but the accounting differs.

A spin-off is accounted for as a dividend. Both the investment account and the retained earnings account are reduced by the book value of the shares distributed. *A split-off is accounted for like a purchase of treasury stock.* The treasury stock account is increased and the equity method investment account is reduced (reflecting the distribution of that asset). The dollar amount recorded for this transaction depends on whether the split-off is a pro rata distribution or a non pro rata distribution.

b. As is the case with all dividends, there is no effect on Bristol Myers' income statement from the spin-off. The assets on Bristol Myers' balance sheet are reduced by the book value of the Zimmer investment and its stockholders' equity is reduced by the same amount through a reduction in retained earnings for the "spin-off" dividend.

M9-32 (10 minutes)

a. A split-off is an exchange of shares between the parent company and its shareholders. In this transaction, AT&T shareholders exchange their shares in the company for AT&T Wireless shares owned by AT&T. This is like AT&T buying its own shares back and using AT&T Wireless shares instead of cash.

b. In a split-off, the parent company can report a gain, equal to the value of the subsidiary in excess of its carrying amount on the balance sheet, if the exchange with its shareholders is not pro rata. By the fact that AT&T reported a gain on the transaction, we can infer that the market value of the AT&T Wireless stock must have been $13.5 billion higher than the carrying value of the AT&T Wireless investment on AT&T's balance sheet at the time of the share exchange.

c. The $13.5 billion gain should be treated as a nonoperating item in our analysis of AT&T for 2003, because it represents a gain on an investment.

EXERCISES

E9-34 (15 minutes)

	Balance Sheet						Income Statement		
Transaction	Cash Asset	+ Noncash Assets	= Liabil-ities	+ Contrib. Capital	+ Earned Capital	Rev-enues	− Expen-ses	= Net Income
Feb 20: Issued 10,000 shares of $1 par value common stock at $25 cash per share	+250,000 Cash		=	+10,000 Common Stock +240,000 Additional Paid-in Capital				
Feb 21: Issued 15,000 shares of $100 par value 8% preferred stock at $275 cash per share	+4,125,000 Cash		=	+1,500,000 Preferred Stock +2,625,000 Additional Paid-in Capita				
Jun 30: Purchased 2,000 shares of common stock at $15 per share	−30,000 Cash		=	−30,000 Treasury Stock				
Sep 25: Sold 1,000 shares of treasury stock at $21 cash per share	+21,000 Cash		=	+15,000 Treasury Stock +6,000 Additional Paid-in Capital				

Left margin notes:

sh 250,000
S 10,000
PIC 240,000

Cash
50,000 |

CS
| 10,000

APIC
| 240,000

sh 4,125,000
S 1,500,000
PIC 2,625,000

Cash
25,000 |

PS
| 1,500,000

APIC
| 2,625,000

30,000
Cash 30,000

TS
30,000 |

Cash
| 30,000

sh 21,000
S 15,000
PIC 6,000

Cash
21,000 |

TS
| 15,000

APIC
| 6,000

E9-36 (20 minutes)

a. Best Buy has issued 485,098,000 shares. At its $0.10 par value, its common stock is recorded at $48,509,800, which is rounded up to $49 million.

b. Best Buy issued shares at an average price of $1.43 per share, computed as ($49 million + $643 million)/ 485,098,000 shares.

c. ($ millions)

Retained earnings, 2/26/2005	$3,315
Net earnings	1,140
Dividends	(151)
Retained earnings, 2/25/2006	$4,304

d. The foreign currency translation adjustment relates to Best Buy's foreign subsidiaries. During the year, the $US equivalent of the foreign subsidiary balance sheets changed because the $US value fluctuated. The $101 million positive amount implies that the $US weakened during the year vis-à-vis the currencies of Best Buy's subsidiaries. Consequently, the net equity of the foreign subsidiaries increased in their $US value, resulting in a positive foreign currency translation adjustment. This adjustment has no effect on Best Buy's reported net earnings until the subsidiary is sold, at which time the balance in the foreign currency translation account relating to that subsidiary is taken into current income.

e. The exercise of employee stock options resulted in the sale of 9 million shares of stock for a total of $257 million ($256 million + $1 million), or at a price of $28.56 per common share. This means Best Buy's common stock increased by 9 million shares x $0.10 par value, or $900,000 (which was rounded up to $1 million). Additional paid-in capital increased for the remainder of $256 million.

f. Best Buy repurchased 18 million shares of common stock for a total of $772 million ($771 million + $1 million), or at a cost of $42.89 per share. The treasury stock account is considered to be a component of contributed (paid-in) capital, and is usually reported separately. When not separately reported, treasury stock would most likely be included, as a reduction, in additional paid-in capital.

E9-38 (20 minutes)

		Distribution to	
		Preferred	**Common**
a.	**Year 1**	$ 0	$ 0
	Year 2: Dividends in arrears from Year 1 ($750,000 × 8%)	$ 60,000	
	Current year dividend ($750,000 × 8%)	60,000	
	Balance to common		$160,000
	Total for Year 2	$120,000	$160,000
	Year 3: Current year dividend ($750,000 × 8%)	$ 60,000	$ 0
b.	**Year 1**	$ 0	$ 0
	Year 2: Current year dividend ($750,000 × 8%)	$ 60,000	
	Balance to common		$220,000
	Year 3: Current year dividend ($750,000 × 8%)	$ 60,000	$ 0

E9-40 (30 minutes)

a.

	Dividend Distribution			
	Preferred	Common	Preferred per Share	Common per Share
2005				
Current year preferred dividends				
[6% × (18,000 × $50)]	$54,000			
Remainder to common		$9,000		
Per share				
Preferred ($54,000 / 18,000)			$3.00	
Common ($9,000 / 90,000)				$0.10
2006				
Preferred	$0		$0.00	
Common		$0		$0.00
2007				
Preferred dividends in arrears				
[6% × (18,000 × $50)]	$54,000			
Current year preferred dividends				
[6% × (18,000 × $50)]	54,000			
Remainder to common		$270,000		
Total distribution	$108,000	$270,000		
Per share				
Preferred ($108,000 / 18,000)			$6.00	
Common ($270,000 / 90,000)				$3.00

E9-40—concluded

b.

	Dividend Distribution			
	Preferred	Common	Preferred per Share	Common per Share
2005				
Preferred	$0		$0.00	
Common		$0		$0.00
2006				
Preferred				
dividends in arrears				
[6% × (18,000 × $50)]	$ 54,000			
Current year preferred				
dividend				
[6% × (18,000 × $50)]	54,000			
Common		$0		
Total distribution	$108,000	$0		
Per share				
Preferred ($108,000 / 18,000)			$6.00	
Common				$0.00
2007				
Current year preferred				
dividend				
[6% × (18,000 × $50)]	$54,000			
Remainder to common		$135,000		
Per share				
Preferred ($54,000 / 18,000)			$3.00	
Common ($135,000 / 90,000)				$1.50

E9-42 (20 minutes)

a.

RE 100,800
CS 56,000
APIC 44,800

		Balance Sheet					Income Statement		
Transaction	Cash Asset	+ Noncash Assets	= Liabil-ities	+ Contrib. Capital	+ Earned Capital	Rev-enues	− Expen-ses	= Net Income
May 12: Declare and issue stock dividend [1]			=	+56,000 Common Stock +44,800 Additional Paid-in Capital	+ −100,800 Retained Earnings			
Dec 31: Declare and pay cash dividend [2]	−64,200 Cash		=		−64,200 Retained Earnings			

RE 100,800
| 100,800

CS
| 56,000

APIC
| 44,800

RE 64,200
Cash 64,200

RE
64,200 |

Cash
| 64,200

[1] The 7% dividend is a small stock dividend and, accordingly, Retained Earnings is reduced by the market value of the shares distributed (7% × 80,000 shares × $18 = $100,800). Common Stock is increased by the par value of the shares ($56,000) and additional paid-in-capital in increased by the remainder ($44,800). After the stock dividend there are 85,600 shares outstanding (80,000 × 1.07).

[2] Retained earnings are reduced by $0.75 per share on 85,600 shares outstanding and cash is decreased by the same amount.

b.

REVSINE COMPANY STATEMENT OF RETAINED EARNINGS FOR YEAR ENDED DECEMBER 31, 2007		
Retained Earnings, December 31, 2006		$305,000
Add: Net Income		283,000
		588,000
Less: Cash Dividends Declared	$ 64,200	
Stock Dividends Declared	100,800	165,000
Retained Earnings, December 31, 2007		$423,000

E9-44 (15 minutes)

a. Immediately after the stock split, 800,000 shares (2 x 400,000 shares) of $10 par value common stock are issued and outstanding.

b. The stock split does not change the Common Stock account balance. The account balance is $8,000,000 just before and immediately after the stock split.

c. The stock split does not change the Paid-in Capital in Excess of Par Value account. The account balance is $3,400,000 just before and immediately after the stock split.

E9-46 (15 minutes)

a. When convertible preferred stock is converted, the balance of the convertible preferred stock is eliminated and total contributed capital (common stock plus additional paid-in capital) is increased by that same amount: Common Stock increases by par value multiplied by the number of shares issued and Additional Paid-In Capital increases by the remainder. In 2002, JetBlue decreased the preferred stock account by $216,394 and increased common stock and APIC by $461 and $215,933 respectively.

b. Employee stock options give employees the right (but not the obligation) to purchase common stock at a pre-set fixed price. In the case of JetBlue, 811,623 shares were issued in return for cash of $1,066,000 ($8,000 + $1,058,000). This increased JetBlue's contributed capital. Specifically, JetBlue received cash equal to the stock options' exercise price and it issued 811,623 common shares to the employees who exercised. This increased Common Stock and Additional Paid-in Capital for the exercise price. Employees purchased shares for an average price of $1.31 per share ($1,066,000 / 811,623 shares). This is a substantial discount from the $20 price range for the stock during 2002.

E9-48 (20 minutes)

a. A split-off involves the exchange of stock that the parent company owns in a subsidiary for the parent company's own shares. The parent company shares acquired are accounted for as treasury stock except instead of cash, the shares of the subsidiary are used in the transaction. If the repurchase is pro rata, the treasury shares are recorded at the book value of the subsidiary shares given up. For example, IMS Health's shareholders would exchange their shares in the company for CTS shares owned by IMS Health. The end result is that IMS Health's shareholders end up owning CTS shares directly rather than indirectly via IMS Health.

b. A gain can only be recorded if the exchange is not pro rata, such as with a general tender offer to accept the shares tendered first, usually up to a maximum number of shares. This is the sort of tender offer IMS Health did announce and execute in 2003.

c. The gain from this split-off relates to a gain arising from an investment. Accordingly, our analysis would consider such a gain as a nonoperating item.

P9-50 (30 minutes)

a.

	Balance Sheet					Income Statement		
Transaction	Cash Asset	+ Noncash Assets	= Liabil-ities	+ Contrib. Capital	+ Earned Capital	Rev-enues	– Expen-ses	= Net Income
Jan 12 [1]								
Sep 1 [2]	–100,000 Cash		=	–100,000 Treasury Stock				
Oct 12 [3]	+18,000 Cash		=	+15,000 Treasury Stock +3,000 Additional Paid-in Capital				
Nov 21 [4]	+55,000 Cash		=	+25,000 Common Stock +30,000 Additional Paid-in Capital				
Dec 28: [5]	+10,800 Cash		=	+12,000 Treasury Stock -1,200 Additional Paid-in Capital				

(margin journal entries, left side)

transaction recorded
100,000
Cash 100,000

TS 100,000
Cash 100,000

h 18,000
S 15,000
PIC 3,000
Cash 18,000

TS 15,000
APIC 3,000

sh 55,000
S 25,000
PIC 30,000
Cash 55,000

CS 25,000
APIC 30,000

sh 10,800
IC 1,200
TS 12,000
Cash 10,800

APIC 1,200
TS 12,000

---

[1] (Memorandum) Common stock split 3 for 1, authorized shares increased to 300,000 and par value reduced to $5 per share.

[2] Cash paid: 10,000 shares × $10 = $100,000. This increases the treasury stock account, which is a contra-equity account that reduces paid-in capital.

[3] Cash received: 1,500 shares × $12 per shares = $18,000. Treasury stock is reduced by its cost of $10 per share and the balance ($3,000) is reflected as an increase in additional paid-in capital.

[4] Cash received: 5,000 shares × $11 per share = $55,000. Common stock increases by the par value (5,000 × $5 = $25,000) and additional paid-in-capital increases by the difference ($30,000).

[5] Cash received: 1,200 shares × $9 = $10,800. Treasury stock is reduced by the cost of the shares (1,200 shares × $10 = $12,000) and APIC is reduced by the remainder ($10,800 - $12,000 = -$1,200).

b.

Stockholders' Equity		
Paid-in capital		
7% Preferred stock, $100 par value, 20,000 shares authorized; 5,000 shares issued and outstanding	$500,000	
Common stock, $5 par value, 300,000 shares authorized; 125,000 shares issued, (7,300 treasury shares)	625,000	$1,125,000
Additional paid-in capital		
Paid-in capital in excess of par value—preferred stock	24,000	
Paid-in capital in excess of par value—common stock	390,000	
Paid-in capital from treasury stock	1,800	415,800
Total paid-in capital		1,540,800
Retained earnings		408,000
		1,948,800
Less: Treasury stock (7,300 common shares) at cost		73,000
Total stockholders' equity		$1,875,800

P9-52 (30 minutes)

		Balance Sheet						Income Statement		
	Transaction	Cash Asset	+ Noncash Assets	= Liabil- ities	+ Contrib. Capital	+ Earned Capital	Rev- enues	− Expen- ses	= Net Income
Cash 62,000 PS 50,000 APIC 12,000 Cash 62,000 | PS | 50,000 APIC | 12,000	Jan. 15 [1]	+62,000 Cash		=	+50,000 Preferred Stock +12,000 Additional Paid-in Capital				
Cash 144,000 CS 80,000 APIC 64,000 Cash 144,000 | CS | 80,000 APIC | 64,000	Jan. 20 [2]	+144,000 Cash		=	+80,000 Common Stock +64,000 Additional Paid-in Capital				
No transaction recorded	May 18 [3]								
Cash 60,000 CS 20,000 APIC 40,000 Cash 60,000 | CS | 20,000 APIC | 40,000	Jun. 1 [4]	+60,000 Cash		=	+20,000 Common Stock +40,000 Additional Paid-in Capital				
45,000 Cash 45,000 TS 45,000 | Cash | 45,000	Sep. 1 [5]	−45,000 Cash		=	−45,000 Treasury Stock				

		Balance Sheet							Income Statement		
Transaction		Cash Asset	+ Noncash Assets	= Liabil-ities	+	Contrib. Capital	+	Earned Capital	Rev-enues	– Expen-ses	= Net Income
Oct. 12 [6]		+18,900 Cash		=		+16,200 Treasury Stock +2,700 Additional Paid-in Capital					
Dec. 22 [7]		+29,500 Cash		=		+25,000 Preferred Stock +4,500 Additional Paid-in Capital					

Cash 18,900
TS 16,200
APIC 2,700

Cash
18,900 |

TS
| 16,200

APIC
| 2,700

Cash 29,500
PS 25,000
APIC 4,500

Cash
29,500 |

PS
| 25,000

APIC
| 4,500

[1] Cash increases by the proceeds from the sale of the preferred stock (1,000 shares × $62 per share = $62,000). The Preferred Stock account is increased for its par value (1,000 shares × $50 par = $50,000) and additional paid-in-capital is increased for the remainder ($12,000).

[2] Cash increases by the proceeds from the sale of the common stock (4,000 shares × $36 = $144,000). Common stock increases by its par value (4,000 × $20 = $80,000) and additional paid-in-capital increases by the remainder ($64,000).

[3] (Memorandum) Common stock split 2 for 1, with authorized shares increased to 100,000 and par value reduced to $10 per share.

[4] After the stock split, the par value is $10. Therefore, common stock increases by $20,000 (2,000 shares × $10 par) and additional paid-in-capital increases by the remainder ($40,000).

[5] Cash decreases by the cost of the treasury stock (2,500 shares × $18 per share = $45,000). Because treasury stock is a contra-equity account, the stock repurchase decreases paid-in-capital.

[6] Cash increases by the proceeds from the sale of the treasury stock (900 × $21 = $18,900). The treasury stock account decreases by the original cost of the shares (900 × $18 = $16,200), thereby increasing paid-in-capital, and additional paid-in-capital increases by the remainder ($2,700).

[7] Cash increases by the proceeds from the sale of the preferred stock (500 × $59 = $29,500). The Preferred Stock account increases for its par value (500 shares × $50 = $25,000) and additional paid-in-capital increases for the remainder ($4,500).

P9-54 (50 minutes)

a. The $2.67 is the amount of dividend per year on each share of Fortune Brand's preferred stock. Preferred stock is typically sold in increments of $100. Thus, the $2.67 implies an initial dividend yield of 2.67%.

b. 229.6 million shares issued × $3.125 par value = $717.5 million; the financial statement reports $717.4 million—the slight difference of $0.1 million is probably due to our use of rounded numbers from the financials.

c. (Common stock + Additional paid-in capital) / Shares issued = Average issue price; computed as ($717.4 million + $182.8 million) / 229.6 million shares = <u>$3.92 per share</u>

d. Fortune Brands reports cumulative foreign exchange translation adjustments of $1.7 million and minimum pension liability adjustments of $(30.3) million as part of its 2005 other comprehensive income adjustments. The accumulated other comprehensive income or loss account also commonly includes unrealized gains and losses from available-for-sale securities and unrealized gains and losses from some hedging activities.

e. Fortune Brands received a dividend from ACCO World Corporation of $613.3 million in conjunction with the spin-off per the footnote. As a result, the carrying amount of its investment was reduced to $(23.5) million ($589.8 million - $613.3 million) per its statement of shareholders' equity. The spin-off, therefore, resulted in an increase in retained earnings as the subsidiary, which had a deficit (negative) stockholders' equity, was distributed to Fortune Brands' shareholders as a dividend.

P9-56 (30 minutes)

a. "Noncumulative" means that any dividends unpaid in one year will not be paid in subsequent years, unpaid dividends are lost to the investor. "Cumulative" means that any unpaid dividends must be paid in full before dividends can be paid to Lucent's common shareholders.

The 8% figure means that, if paid, the dividends will equal 8% of the stock's par value. Of course, dividends are not a contractual obligation – they depend on the company having sufficient cash and cash inflows.

"Convertible" means that the preferred stock can be exchanged for common stock. Usually this option rests with the holder of the preferred stock. Sometimes, companies can retain an option to force the conversion. This is spelled out in the preferred stock contract.

The "liquidation preference" indicates the amount that will be paid to the preferred shareholders in the event that Lucent fails. This amount must be paid in full before the common shareholders can be paid anything in the event of Lucent's liquidation or dissolution.

b. When Lucent issued the preferred shares, both cash and contributed capital increased by the issue price. Specifically: Cash and Contributed Capital both increased by $1.8 billion. The sale of convertible preferred stock is accounted for like the sale of preferred stock that is not convertible; that is, the conversion feature is not accounted for separately unless it is detachable and can be sold as a separate security.

c. (1) If Lucent redeems the preferred stock for cash, the cash account and the preferred stock account are reduced by the same amount.

(2) If the preferred stock is converted into common, the preferred stock is removed from the balance sheet and the common stock is added. That is, the contributed capital (common stock and additional paid-in capital) accounts increase as if the common stock were sold for cash equal to the book value of the preferred stock.

d. We must consider convertible preferred shares in our analysis as the potential shares to be issued represent a contingent claim on the future company's cash flows. Convertible preferred shares affect the computation of diluted EPS, which assumes conversion at the earliest possible opportunity. The foregone preferred dividends are added back to the EPS numerator, and the additional shares issued are added to the denominator. The net effect is a reduction in the diluted EPS over basic EPS.

9-58 (20 minutes)

Companies can recognize gains on split-offs. In general, split-offs result in a gain equal to the excess of the market price of the subsidiary's (split-off) shares in excess of their carrying amount on the parent's books, provided that the split-off is structured as a non-pro rata distribution. To the extent that an unrecognized gain exists and the firm's compensation plan is based on reported profits, managers might deliberately structure the transaction as a non-pro rata split-off in order to realize increased bonus payments. As far as governance, companies can anticipate this activity by excluding gains of this type from the income on which bonuses are computed.

Module 10

Reporting and Analyzing Off-Balance-Sheet Financing

QUESTIONS

Q10-2. The lease footnote provides sufficient information to allow for capitalization of operating leases for analysis purposes. Despite the quality of the lease disclosures, on-balance sheet treatment is, arguably, a more direct form of communication from the company and, as a result, is more easily interpreted by users of its financial statements.

Q10-4. Under defined contribution plans, companies make contributions to the plans which, together with earnings on the amounts invested, provide the sole source of funding for payments to retirees. Under defined benefit plans, companies are obligated to make future payments whose amount and timing is defined by the rules of the pension plan. Pension payments typically depend on an employee's years of service and pay level. Defined benefit plans may or may not be fully funded. Since the company's obligation is extinguished upon payment for a defined contribution plan, the accounting is relatively simple: record an expense when paid or accrued. Defined benefit plans present a number of complications in that the liability is very difficult to estimate and involves several critical assumptions. In addition, companies lobbied for (and the FASB agreed to) various mechanisms to smooth the impact of pension costs on reported earnings. These smoothing mechanisms further complicate the accounting for defined benefit plans vis-à-vis defined contribution plans. (Note: the FASB is considering amending the pension standard to eliminate these smoothing mechanisms.)

Q10-6. Service cost, interest cost and the expected return on plan investments (a reduction of the pension cost) are the basic components of pension expense. Companies might also report amortization of deferred gains and losses should these exceed prescribed limits.

Q10-8. Special purpose entities, SPEs are typically used to securitize assets or to provide project financing. Examples include selling (securitizing) receivables and other assets, acquiring or leasing real estate or other manufacturing assets. In some cases, a SPE can be classified as a Variable Interest Entity (VIE). The "primary beneficiary" of the VIE is the party that realizes most of the benefits from the VIE and bears most of the VIE's risks of failure. It is this entity that is required to consolidate the VIE on its balance sheet, thus increasing its assets and liabilities.

©Cambridge Business Publishers, 2008

M10-10 (15 minutes)

a. YUM records its capital leases on the balance sheet -- both the leased asset and the lease liability. By contrast, YUM's operating leases are not on the balance sheet. Operating leases are, as a result, a common technique to achieve off-balance sheet financing. YUM's income statement includes depreciation of the capital leased asset and interest expense on the capital lease liability. YUM's operating leases result in rent expense.

b. Analysts frequently add the present value of the future operating lease payments to both assets and liabilities, thus capitalizing the operating lease. The company's asset turnover will, therefore, be lower, and its financial leverage (total liabilities-to-equity ratio) higher. Analysis of the income statement involves removing rent expense and adding depreciation and interest expense. NOPAT will, therefore, increase because depreciation expense will be less than rent expense.

M10-12 (15 minutes)

a. American Express reports $112 million in pension expense for 2005. The footnote also reports the component parts of the total expense.

b. Expected returns on plan assets offset service and interest costs and reduce reported pension expense. In 2005, expected returns reduced American Express' pension expense by $141.

c. "Expected" refers to companies' use of long-term average returns on the investment portfolio. Expected returns are used in the computation of pension expense, rather than actual returns. This results in smoother pension expense and thus, smoother reported income.

M10-14 (15 minutes)

a. The actual return on plan assets ($63 million) has no effect on profits for the year. Only the <u>estimated return</u> affects the pension expense that YUM! reports on its income statement. The actual return on plan assets does affect the balance of the plan assets.

b. YUM! cash outflow relate to the <u>company contributions</u> of $64 million (assuming that these contributions are made with cash and not with stock). The benefits paid reduce the pension plan's assets, but are not a cash outflow for the company.

c. The benefit payments of $33 million reduce the pension liability, the PBO.

M10-16 (15 minutes)

a. Dow established these variable interest entities (VIEs) to acquire certain assets and lease them back to Dow, where Dow would record them as operating leases. In that way Dow is able to utilize the assets of the VIE without recording the asset values and any related liabilities. Dow would only record the "rent expense" from the leases. This is classic off-balance-sheet financing. Dow likely expects that this structure lowers the cost of capital by reducing the company's perceived financial leverage.

b. Prior to passage of FIN46(R), companies were not required to consolidate VIEs. In its 2002 report, Dow refers to "operating leases" associated with its various special purpose entities. Dow's classification of these leases as "operating" means that neither the lease asset nor the lease liability appear on Dow's balance sheet. The leases represent off-balance-sheet financing of Dow. (If unchanged, Dow would have needed to consolidate these leases by the third quarter of 2003.)

FIN46(R) required primary beneficiaries to consolidate their VIEs. In its 2005 report, Dow discloses that it restructured those leases. After restructuring, Dow determined that it was not the primary beneficiary of the "owner trust" in control of the leases. Accordingly, consolidation was not required in 2005.

Consequently, while the rules governing consolidation of VIEs differ, the effect of Dow's accounting treatment is similar for both 2003 and 2005; that is, the lease assets and obligations remain off-balance sheet.

c. FIN46(R) requires that the "primary beneficiary" consolidate the VIE. The primary beneficiary is the entity that enjoys most of the benefits from the VIE's activities and bears most of the risk if the VIE performs poorly. Consolidation combines the balance sheets of the two entities (Dow and the VIE). In that event, the lease asset and lease liabilities (of approximately $394) would appear on Dow's balance sheet. This consolidation would negate the off-balance-sheet benefits that Dow presently enjoys by virtue of the operating lease treatment.

d. It is reasonable to assume that Dow wanted to avoid consolidating the owner trust assets and liabilities. This possibility seems likely since Dow must still maintain the residual value guarantee and did not disclose any other changes to the lease structure. There is no other plausible reason for the lease restructuring.

M10-18 (15 minutes)

a. The funded status is ($4,989) – negative, which indicates an underfunded pension plan. It is, therefore, reported as a long-term liability under current GAAP on Lockheed's balance sheet.

b. The negative funded status represents the present value of expected pension benefit payments to retirees in excess of the current funds available to pay those benefits. It is a long-term liability that should be treated no differently from other debt obligations. Our analysis, therefore, focuses on the company's ability to repay the obligations when they mature.

c. Lockheed is significantly more financially leveraged than the average company, with a total liabilities-to-equity ratio of 2.5:1 calculated as, [($27.7-$7.9) / $7.9] billion). The average total liabilities-to-equity ratio for publicly traded companies is about 1:1.

d. Lockheed generates a significant amount of operating cash flow, much greater than its capital expenditures. This yields a high level of free cash flow, and tempers, to some extent, our negative impression of Lockheed's financial leverage in part (c). Still, we need to monitor its other debt obligations to gain comfort that it will be able to generate enough cash to meet its total payment requirements (debt and pension).

EXERCISES

E10-20 (20 minutes)

a. According to Verizon's lease footnote, it has both capital and operating leases. Only the capital leases are reported on-balance-sheet in the amount of $112 million ($17 million in current liabilities and $95 million as long-term liabilities). However, this is not Verizon's total lease obligation. Verizon also has sizeable leases that it has classified as operating. In fact, the minimum lease payments under operating leases are over 27 times that for capital leases--$4,497 million vis-à-vis $166 million! These operating leases are not reported on-balance-sheet.

b. Neither the lease asset nor the lease obligation is reported on the balance sheet for an operating lease. As a result, total assets and total liabilities are lower than if the lease had been classified as capital. Over the lease term, total rent expense under operating leases will be equal to the interest and depreciation expense that the company would record under capital leases. Cumulative profit over the life of the leases is unaffected by this classification. In any particular year during the lease, however, the two will not be equal. Even if depreciation is computed on a straight-line basis, interest is accrued based on the balance of the lease obligation which is higher in the earlier years of the lease. As a result, depreciation plus interest will exceed rent expense during the early years of the lease life and will be less toward the end of the lease. However, these differences tend to be small for most leases.

c.

Year ($ millions)	Operating Lease Payment	Discount Factor (i=0.10)	Present Value
1	$1,184	0.90909	$1,076
2	791	0.82645	654
3	652	0.75131	490
4	504	0.68301	344
5	316	0.62092	196
>5	1,050	2.48685* x 0.62092	488**
Remaining life....	3.323 years		$3,248

* Present value of an annuity of 3 years at 10%
** $316 x 2.48685 x 0.62092 = $488
** $1,050 ÷ $316 per year = 3.323 years, rounded to 3 years

(Alternate solution using present value formula or financial calculator: Present value of annuity factor for 3.323 years at 10% = 2.71462; $316 x 2.71462 x 0.62092 = $533; Total present value = $3,293)

The present value of its operating leases is $3,248 million, see above table. To assess the company's financial condition and performance, based on all of the company's assets and liabilities, we might add the present value of its operating leases to both assets and liabilities. Further, to adjust the income statement, we can replace rent expense with the depreciation of the lease assets and interest on the lease liability. These adjusted numbers would serve at the basis of a more accurate analysis.

E10-22 (25 minutes)

a. Our analysis might capitalize (add to both assets and liabilities) the present value of the expected operating lease payments. Assuming a 7% discount rate, the present value of lease obligation and asset is computed as follows:

Year ($ millions)	Operating Lease Payment	Discount Factor (i=0.07)	Present Value
1	$ 362	0.93458	$ 338
2	326	0.87344	285
3	286	0.81630	233
4	258	0.76290	197
5	230	0.71299	164
>5	1,218	4.10020*	672**
Remaining life	5.296 years***		$1,889

* Present value of an annuity of 5 periods at 7%
** $230 x 4.10020 x 0.71299 = $672
*** $1,218 ÷ $230 per year = 5.296 years, rounded to 5 years

(Alternate solution using present value formula or a financial calculator: Present value of annuity factor for 5.296 years at 7% = 4.30215; $230 x 4.30215 x 0.71299 = $705; Total present value = $1,922)

Explanation: Thus, the present value of YUM's operating leases is computed to be $1,889 million. This suggests we adjust its balance sheet by adding this amount to both assets and liabilities. Further, to adjust the income statement, we can replace rent expense with the depreciation of the lease assets and interest on the lease liability.

b. YUM!'s liabilities would be 45% higher following the adjustment suggested in part a. Specifically, its adjusted liabilities would total $6,138 million, computed as $4,249 million reported + $1,889 million adjustment. Commensurate with the liability adjustment, we would also adjust its assets figure by $1,889 million for YUM!'s off-balance-sheet lease assets.

E10-24 (20 minutes)

a. Service cost represents the additional pension benefits earned by employees during the current year but paid to employees in the future.

Interest cost is an expense that accrues on the pension obligation (PBO) during the year.

b. During fiscal 2005, retirees received payments totaling $2,856 million for U.S. pension plans and $1,355 million for non-U.S. pension plans. These payments came from the pension plan assets and not from Ford's operating cash flows.

c. Funded status is defined as the pension obligation less the fair market value of the pension investments. In this case the funded status of the U.S. pension plans is computed as: $43,895 million (pension obligation) – $41,857 million (pension asset) = $(2,038) million. Its non-U.S. plans are underfunded by $8,773 million ($30,700 million - $21,927 million).

d. Actuarial gains (losses) are decreases (increases) to the PBO resulting from changes in the *assumptions* used to estimate the pension or health care liability. The assumptions include the expected wage inflation rate, mortality and termination rates, and the discount rate used to compute the present value of the obligation.

Plan amendment adjustments are changes to the liability arising from amendments to the plan itself, such as the level of benefits, qualifications of employees eligible to receive benefits, or the period of time over which benefits will be paid.

e. Ford generates a significant amount of operating cash flow, three times its capital expenditures. Nevertheless, the free cash flow of $19.6 billion ($27.1 billion - $7.5 billion) is not a significant multiple of the $4,240 ($2,870 million + $1,370 million) of expected benefit payments to pension retirees in 2006 alone. Given the underfunded status of the plans, Ford will likely need to significantly increase its pension contributions in the future in order to maintain the solvency of its plans. We need to monitor its other debt obligations closely to gain comfort that it will be able to generate enough cash to meet its total payment requirements (debt and pension).

E10-26 (20 minutes)

a. <u>Service cost</u> represents the additional pension benefits earned by employees during the current year but paid to employees in the future.

<u>Interest cost</u> is an expense that accrues on the pension obligation (PBO) during the year.

b. During 2005, retirees were paid $2,977 million for pensions and $1,706 million for health care. These payments were made from the pension and health care plans' assets. There is a corresponding reduction in the related obligations.

The company does not pay retirees directly. Payments to retirees are made from the pension and health care investment accounts.

c. The funded status is the difference between the obligation and the fair market value of the plan assets. For Verizon, the funded status of its pension plan is $3,429 million ($40,990 million plan assets - $37,561 million PBO). This implies an overfunded pension plan.

However, Verizon's health care plan is underfunded by $23,533 million ($27,809 million obligation less $4,276 million assets).

d. Verizon reports pension *income* of $366 million, resulting primarily from the overfunded nature of its pension plan.

It reports an expense of $2,104 million relating to its health care plan.

e. Actuarial gains (losses) are decreases (increases) to the PBO resulting form changes in the *assumptions* used to estimate the pension or health care liability. The assumptions include the expected wage inflation rate, mortality and termination rates, and the discount rate used to compute the present value of the obligation. Plan amendment adjustments are changes to the liability arising from amendments to the plan itself, such as the level of benefits, qualifications of employees to receive benefits, or the period of time over which benefits will be paid.

PROBLEMS

P10-28 (40 minutes)

a. All of Abercrombie & Fitch's leases are classified as operating. GAAP requires companies to provide a table of future lease payments for both operating and capital leases when they exist. Because no capital leases are included in the Abercrombie & Fitch footnote, we know that it only has operating leases. Because operating leases are not capitalized on the balance sheet, neither lease assets nor lease liabilities appear on the Abercrombie & Fitch balance sheets.

b. Total assets and total liabilities for Abercrombie are lower than if the operating leases had been capitalized. Over the life of the lease, total rent expense under operating leases is equal to the interest and depreciation expense that is recorded under capital leases. Total profit is unaffected by this classification. In any particular year during the life of the lease, however, income is not the same under both methods. Even if depreciation is computed on a straight-line basis, interest is accrued based on the balance of the lease obligation, which is higher in the earlier years of the lease. As a result, depreciation plus interest will exceed rent expense during the early years of the lease life and will be less toward the end of the lease. However, these differences tend to be small for most leases. (Note: NOPAT excludes interest expense from capital leases.)

c. Using a 7% discount rate, we can calculate the present value of A&F's operating lease payments. Each of the first 5 years' projected lease payments is discounted individually. Then, the payments due after 5 years represent a 3.46 year annuity based on the year 5 payment amount, rounded to 3 years so that we can use the tables. The present value of this annuity is, then, discounted from year 5 to the present. The sum of the present values is approximately $1.016 billion, computed as follows:

P10-28—continued

c. Continued.

Year ($ 000s)	Operating Lease Payment	Discount Factor (i=0.07)	Present Value
1......................	$187,674	0.93458	$ 175,396
2......................	187,397	0.87344	163,680
3......................	178,595	0.81630	145,787
4......................	169,856	0.76290	129,583
5......................	155,670	0.71299	110,991
>5......................	538,635	2.62432* x 0.71299	291,276**
Remaining life...	3.460*** years		$1,016,713

*Present value of an annuity for 3 years at 7%
** $155,670 x 2.62432 x 0.71299 = $291,276
***$538,635 ÷ $155,670 per year = 3.46 years, rounded to 3 years.

(Alternate solution using present value formula or financial calculator:
Present value of annuity factor for 3.46 years at 7% = 2.98166;
$155,670 x 2.98166 x 0.71299 = $330,785; Total present value = $1,056,222)

d. Capitalization of Abercrombie & Fitch's operating leases would increase operating profit by $60,585. In particular, A&F would make the following adjustments to its income statement:
  1. Remove rent expense of $187,674
  2. Add depreciation expense of $1,016,713 / 8 years = $127,089.
(note: in addition, interest expense of $1,016,713 × 7% = $71,170 would be recognized as a nonoperating expense)

e. Failure to report the lease assets and lease obligation on-balance-sheet overstates asset turnover (NOAT) because significant assets are omitted from A&F's balance sheet; and understates financial leverage because significant liabilities are omitted. The net operating profit margin (NOPM) will be understated by the use of operating leases, as rent expense is greater than the depreciation expense that would have been recognized had the leases been capitalized. In sum, if these leases are capitalized: NOAT is lower, NOPM is higher and leverage is higher. Net income would be lower if the leases are capitalized because the sum of depreciation expense ($127,089) and interest expense ($71,170) is $198,259 which is greater than the rent expense of $187,674. Thus, ROE would be lower if A&F capitalized the leases.

©Cambridge Business Publishers, 2008

P10-30 (40 minutes)

a. FedEx's lease footnote reveal that it has both capital and operating leases. However, only capital leases are reported on-balance-sheet; those leases are reported in the amount of $401 million. FedEx would also report a lease asset on its balance sheet, but that asset is likely to carry a different balance than the $401 million lease liability due to depreciation, etc.

The $401 million for capital leases is not the total obligation to its lessors. FedEx also has sizeable leases classified as operating. It footnotes reveal that the minimum lease payments under operating leases totals $14,005 million, which is about 35 times greater than the capital lease payments of $401 million! FedEx's operating leases are not reported on-balance-sheet.

b. We can impute the discount rate FedEx uses to compute the present value of its capital leases by trial-and-error. The analysis in the following table reveals that FedEx is using a discount rate of approximately 3%.

Year ($ millions)	Capital Lease Payment	Discount Factor (i=0.03)	Present Value
1	$121	0.97087	$117
2	22	0.94260	21
3	99	0.91514	91
4	11	0.88849	10
5	96	0.86261	83
>5	130	0.97087* x 0.86261	80**
Remaining life	1.354 years		$402

   * Present value of an annuity of 1 year at 3%.
   ** $96 x 0.97087 x 0.86261 = $80 (rounded).
   *** $130 ÷ $96 per year = 1.354 years, rounded to 1 year so that tables can be used.

    (An alternate solution is to use a financial calculator and solve for IRR with the following inputs: $CF_0 = -401$, $CF_1 = 121$, $CF_2 = 22$, $CF_3 = 99$, $CF_4 = 11$, $CF_5 = 96$, $CF_6 = 96$, $CF_7 = 34$. This yields IRR = 2.99%.)

P10-30—continued

c. Using a 3% discount rate, the present value of FedEx's operating lease payments is computed to be $11,845 million as follows:

Year ($ millions)	Operating Lease Payment	Discount Factor (i=0.03)	Present Value
1	$1,646	0.97087	$ 1,598
2	1,518	0.94260	1,431
3	1,356	0.91514	1,241
4	1,191	0.88849	1,058
5	1,045	0.86261	901
>5	7,249	6.23028* x 0.86261	5,616**
Remaining life....	6.937 years		$11,845

*   Present value of an annuity of 7 years at 3%
** $1,045 x 6.23028 x 0.86261 = $5,616
*** $7,249 ÷ $1,045 per year = 6.937 years, rounded to 7 years so the tables can be used.

(Alternate solution using present value formula or financial calculator: Present value of annuity factor for 6.937 years @ 3% = 6.17976; $1,045 x 6.17976 x 0.86261 = $5,571; Total present value = $11,800)

Explanation: Each of the first 5 years' projected lease payment is discounted individually. Then, the payments due after 5 years represent a 6.937-year annuity based on the year 5 payment amount, rounded to 7 years so that tables can be used. The present value of this annuity is, then, discounted from year 5. The sum of the present values is approximately $11,845 million.

d. Capitalization of FedEx's operating leases would increase operating profit in fiscal 2006 by $659. In particular, FedEx would make the following adjustments to its income statement:
 1. Remove rent expense of $1,646 million
 2. Add depreciation expense of $11,845 million / 12 years = $987 million.
 (note: interest expense of $11,845 million x 3% = $355 million would be recognized as well as a nonoperating expense)

e. Failure to report the lease assets and lease obligation on-balance-sheet overstates asset turnover (NOAT) because significant assets are omitted from FedEx's balance sheet; and understates financial leverage because significant liabilities are omitted. The net operating profit margin (NOPM) will be understated by the use of operating leases, as rent expense is greater than the depreciation expense that would have been recognized had the leases been capitalized. Our conclusion of the underlying source of the ROE performance is markedly affected, as we can now see that FedEx is achieving its ROE with lower turnover and higher financial leverage than was apparent based on our review of the published (unadjusted) financial statements. In sum, if these leases are capitalized: NOAT is lower, NOPM is higher (interest expense is nonoperating), and leverage is higher.

f. FedEx reports $401 million of capitalized leases on-balance-sheet. Another $11,845 million of lease assets and related lease obligations is off-balance-sheet as operating leases. Consequently, about 3.3% of FedEx's total leases are reported on-balance-sheet [$401 ÷ ($401 + $11,845)].

g. There are sizeable assets that FedEx requires to conduct its business that are not reported on-balance-sheet. Thus, the actual extent of FedEx's required investment and related operating obligations is markedly understated. It appears, therefore, that the balance sheet for FedEx does not do an adequate job at reporting the company's economic assets and liabilities.

P10-32 (50 minutes)

a. Dow Chemical reported pension expense of <u>$187 million</u> for 2005. (It also reported other postretirement expense of $130 million.)

b. The expected return is computed as the beginning fair market value of the pension plan assets multiplied by the long-term expected return on these investments. For 2005, this is computed as $12,206 million × 8.75% = <u>$1,068 million</u>, slightly higher than the reported amount of $1,056 million.

In contrast to the $1,056 million of expected return on plan assets that is used in computing pension expense for 2005, plan assets report an *actual gain* of $877 million.

If Dow used actual returns instead of expected returns, company profits would fluctuate with investment-market swings. The logic behind using the long-term expected rate is that investment returns are expected to fluctuate around this average and its use would more accurately capture the average cost of the pension plan. It is similar to the logic of reporting held-to-maturity debt securities at historical cost rather than current market value.

c. Its pension liability is increased by $279 million in service costs and $815 million in interest costs and decreased by $808 million in payments made to plan participants. During 2005, Dow revised the actuarial assumptions used to compute its pension liability, including either a change in the discount rate and/or the rate of expected wage inflation. These changes increased Dow's pension liability by $698 million.

The pension plan assets increased by $877 million from actual investment gains and increased by $1,031 million from Dow's contributions during the year. The plan assets decreased by $808 million for benefits paid to plan participants.

d. "Funded status" refers to the excess (deficiency) of the pension obligation over plan assets. If plan assets exceed the pension obligation, the funded status is positive. If plan assets are less than the pension obligation, the funded status is negative.

Dow Chemical's pension plan is <u>underfunded by $2,293 million</u> at the end of 2005. Pension obligations are $15,617 million and pension assets are $13,324 million.

Dow's health care plan is almost entirely unfunded ($1,791 million). Health care obligations amount to $2,168 million, while plan assets are $377 million. Companies typically do not fund health care obligations unless they receive a tax benefit from contributions or it is required by law.

©Cambridge Business Publishers, 2008

e. *Balance sheet effect:* Since the pension obligation is computed as the present value of expected future pension payments, a reduction in the discount rate increases the present value of that obligation reported on the balance sheet.

Income statement effect: The effect on the income statement is more difficult to predict. The interest cost component of pension expense is the product of the beginning of the year pension obligation and the discount rate. The effect of a reduction in the discount rate is to apply a lower discount rate to a higher pension obligation. These two effects are offsetting and it is not clear which will dominate. (We might also view these effects as follows: (i) discount rate↓, (ii) discount rate↓→PBO↑, applying simple PV logic, and (iii) since Interest cost = Discount rate x PBO, we see a lower discount rate multiplied by a larger PBO, yielding an ambiguous result for interest cost.

f. The decrease in expected return unambiguously decreases profitability because pension cost is increased. This is because the long-term rate is used to compute the dollar amount of expected return that is applied to offset pension expense.

g. Dow's cash flow was affected by the company's contribution of <u>$1,031 million cash</u> to its pension plan. During 2005, Dow did not pay any cash to its health care plan.

Note that the cash payment of benefits to retirees is made from plan assets and does <u>not</u> have a direct effect on Dow's cash flow. Only the contributions to the pension plan affect the company's cash flow.

Module 11

Adjusting and Forecasting Financial Statements

QUESTIONS

Q11-2. Adjusting the income statement involves 1) removing transitory items, 2) separating operating and nonoperating items, and 3) adding expenses not reflected in income. Examples of transitory items include gains (losses) on sales or write-downs of assets, items reported "below the line," that is, below income from continuing operations (discontinued operations, extraordinary items, and changes in accounting principles), restructuring expenses, lawsuit gains and losses, acquisition-related costs, and others. Nonoperating income (expense) items include financial income (expense) and income (expense) related to discontinued operations. Adding expenses not reflected in income can include stock option expense (prior to 2006), inadequate warranty and other reserves, and reductions of operating activities that result in current expense, such as advertising, R&D and the like.

Q11-4. Adjusting the statement of cash flows involves the proper classification of cash flows relating to operating, investing and financing activities. For example, companies frequently securitize assets, and many analysts consider this to be a financing activity even though the asset reduction is often classified as an operating activity. Another issue relates to the generation of operating cash flows via changes in operating activities that may lead to a short-term gain at a longer-term cost. Examples include reducing expenditures relating to advertising, R&D, and increases in operating cash flows resulting from excessive receivable and inventory reductions and excessive "leaning on the trade" (delaying payment of accounts payable beyond a period considered to be customary).

Q11-6. Many analysts adjust the financial statements before forecasting future results. This adjusting process typically entails eliminating transitory items from the income statement, adjusting the balance sheet to recognize unrecorded assets and liabilities, and examining the statement of cash flows to identify (and adjust for) operating cash flow implications of working capital levels that are perceived to be too low and increases to operating cash flow resulting from asset securitizations and exercises of employee stock options.

Q11-8. We are typically interested in forecasting year-end balances not yearly averages. Using year-end balances to compute historic turnover rates allows us to use the turnover ratio to forecast year-end balances. If we use the typical turnover rate

©Cambridge Business Publishers, 2008

definition, with account averages in the denominator, those turnover rates will forecast the *average* balance for the account.

Q11-10. In the first step, balance sheet items are forecasted using forecasted sales and cost of goods sold (COGS) and other relevant turnover ratios. Long-term assets are forecasted using forecasted capital expenditures. Long-term liabilities are forecasted from current maturities of long-term debt disclosed in the debt footnote, and paid-in-capital is assumed to be constant in this stage. Retained earnings are forecasted by adding (subtracting) forecasted profits (losses) and subtracting forecasted dividends. Once total liabilities and equities are forecasted, total assets is set equal to this amount and forecasted cash is computed as the balancing figure. In the second step, long-term liabilities and equities are adjusted to yield the desired level of cash. The analyst must be careful to maintain the historical leverage ratio and adjust marketable securities or liabilities and equities proportionately.

MINI EXERCISES

M11-12 (20 minutes)

Forecast assumptions as provided in the textbook are:

Revenue growth 12.4%

Gross profit margin.. 25.0%

Selling, general and administrative expense / Revenue 19.7%

Income tax expense / Earnings from continuing
    operations before income tax.. 33.8%

($ millions)					2007
Revenue	(	$30,848	x	1.124)	$ 34,673
Cost of Goods Sold	(	$34,673	x	75.0%)	26,005
Gross Profit	(	$34,673	x	25.0%)	8,668
Selling, general and administrative expense..	(	$34,673	x	19.7%)	6,831
Operating income					1,838
Net Interest income.....................................	(	no change		)	(77)
Earnings from continuing operations before income tax					1,915
Income tax expense....................................	(	1,915	x	33.8%)	647
Net earnings					$ 1,268

M11-14 (15 minutes)

a.

Recall that:

Net operating working capital turnover = Sales / Net operating working capital

Net operating long-term asset turnover = Sales / Net operating long-term assets

Forecasted net operating working capital	Forecasted net operating long-term assets
$6,051 million/ 2.38 = $2,542 million	$6,051 million / 6.99 = $866 million

b. Harley reports a significant amount of financing receivables on its balance sheet. These are notes and leases receivable. These receivables generally take a longer time to collect than typical receivables, thus reducing the working capital turnover rate.

M11-16 (10 minutes)

a. The negative balance for cash indicates that the company is going to require additional financing in the coming year.

b. Given a negative cash balance, the next step would be to increase long-term debt and/or equity or decrease marketable securities on the forecasted balance sheet. Unless you are forecasting a change in the financial leverage of the company (which we would be reluctant to do), long-term debt and equity should be increased in the same proportion of total capital as calculated for the current year.

M11-18 (15 minutes)

The loss on the disposal of the three European generic pharmaceutical businesses represents discontinued operations. As such, the loss of $3 million is a transitory item and is not included in the forecasted income statement, other than the possible investment returns on any cash or securities received from the sale of the businesses. Discontinued operations are sometimes separated in the balance sheet. If so, we should treat them as nonoperating assets and liabilities. Further, in our projections, the assets and liabilities of these operations should be replaced by the assets received in their disposition. The cash flow from investing activities will include the cash proceeds of $5.6 million. These should not be considered persistent cash flows when we forecast future cash flows. Consequently, you should remove them from the statement of cash flows in the adjustment stage.

EXERCISES

E11-20 (25 minutes)

($ millions)		2006
Operating activities		
Net income.. (from E11-19)		$ 165
Depreciation .... ($1,055 x 15.3%)		161
Trade accounts receivable.................. ($67 - $81)		(14)
Merchandise inventories..................... ($174 - $212)		(38)
Trade accounts payable .... ($125 - $103)		22
Accrued payroll, bonus and other ..... ($154 - $127)		27
Net cash flow from operating activities....................................		324
Investing activities		
PPE (net) .... (computed*)		(389)
Net cash flow from investing activities....................................		(389)
Financing activities		
Long-term debt................................ (prior year CMLTD)		(6)
Dividends....................................... (computed **)		(62)
Net cash flows from financing activities....................................		(69)
Net change in cash		(134)
Beginning cash		346
Ending cash......................................		$ 212

* Beginning PPE $1,055 - Ending PPE $1,283 - Depreciation $161
** Dividends $66 – Increase in dividends payable $4

E11-22

Abercrombie & Fitch Statement of Cash Flows

($ thousands)				2007
Operating activities				
Net income......................................	(from E11-21		) $	459,012
Depreciation	($813,603 x	18.1%)		147,262
Receivables	($41,855 -	$57,678)		(15,823)
Inventories....................................	($362,536 -	$500,197)		(137,661)
Accounts Payable........................	($119,249 -	$86,572)		32,677
Accrued Expenses.......................	($296,319 -	$215,034)		81,285
Income taxes payable..................	($136,725 -	$99,480)		37,245
Net cash flow from operating activities..................................				603,997
Investing activities				
Property and Equipment, net.....	(computed*		)	(455,686)
Net cash flow from investing activities..................................				(455,686)
Financing activities				
Dividends......................................				(52,218)
Net cash flows from financing activities..................................				(52,218)
Net change in cash				96,093
Beginning cash				50,687
Ending cash..................................			$	146,780

* Beginning PPE $813,603 - Ending PPE $1,122,027 - Depreciation $147,262

E11-24 (30 minutes)

Best Buy Statement of Cash Flows

($ millions)						2007
Net earnings .... (	from E11-23			)	$	1,268
Depreciation .... (	2,712	x	18.5%	)		502
Receivables .... (	506	-	569	)		(63)
Merchandise inventories.......... (	3,338	-	3,753	)		(415)
Accounts Payable...................... (	3,637	-	3,234	)		403
Accrued Expenses.................... (	1,385	-	1,232	)		153
Income taxes payable............... (	783	-	703	)		80
Net cash flow from operating activities................................						1,928
PPE (net) .... (	computed***			)		(838)
Net cash flow from investing activities................................						(838)
Long-term debt.......................... (	prior year CMLTD			)		(418)
Dividends................................... (	1,264	x	13.2%	)		(167)
Net cash flows from financing activities..............						(585)
Net change in cash						505
Beginning cash						681
Ending cash...............................					$	1,186

*** Beginning PPE $2,712 – Ending PPE $3,048 – Depreciation $502

E11-26 (30 minutes)

($ millions)					2007
Operating activities					
Net income.............................. (	from E11-25			)	$ 1,132
Depreciation .... (	$2,997	x	14.1%	)	423
Receivables .... (	$1,076	-	$1,113	)	(37)
Inventories.............................. (	$1,055	-	$1,092	)	(37)
Accounts Payable................... (	$1,191	-	$1,151	)	40
Other current liabilities .... (	$1,401	-	$1,353	)	48
Net cash flow from operating activities..............................					1,569
Investing activities					
PPE (net) .... (	computed*			)	(531)
Net cash flow from investing activities..............................					(531)
Financing activities					
Long-term debt...................... (	Prior year CMLTD			)	(2,131)
Dividends................................ (	$1,132	x	44.5%		(504)
Net cash flows from financing activities..............................					(2,635)
Net change in cash					(1,597)
Beginning cash					647
Ending cash................................					$ (950)

*   Beginning PPE $2,997 – Ending PPE $3,105 – Depreciation $423 (rounded)

E11-28 (20 minutes)

One adjustment you might consider is to consolidate the TAP joint venture for analysis purposes. This process involves the following steps:

1. Eliminate the investment account of $167 million from Abbott Laboratories' balance sheet

2. Add TAP's assets of $1,470.2 million and liabilities of $1,136.2 million to Abbott Laboratories' balance sheet together with a Minority (Noncontrolling) Interest balance of $167 million (50% of TAP's equity that Abbott does not own. Minority interest is typically treated as an Equity account for analysis purposes).

The Abbott Laboratories footnotes, as is typical, do not provide information relating to the composition of TAP's assets and liability accounts. As a result, we do not know the operating/nonoperating breakdown of either the assets or liabilities. A conservative approach would be to treat the assets as operating and the liabilities as nonoperating. This would result in the maximum amount of net operating assets.

TAP, and its other joint venture partner, Takeda Pharmaceutical Company, Limited of Japan, have equal investments in the TAP joint venture. The extent of their respective liabilities will be spelled out in the joint venture agreement. Abbott Laboratories may have a moral obligation to support TAP that may exceed its legal liability, especially if this venture is important strategically and/or Abbott Laboratories intends to use this financing structure for future ventures. That is, Abbott Laboratories may find it hard to walk away from a failing business, even if it can legally, when the market knows that it is involved.

E11-30 (25 minutes)

| $ millions | 2006 | Forecast Horizon | | | |
		2007 Est.	2008 Est.	2009 Est.	2010 Est.
Sales*	$14,380	$17,529 ($14,380 * 1.219)	$21,368 ($17,529 * 1.219)	$26,048 ($21,368 * 1.219)	$31,753 ($26,048 * 1.219)
NOPAT**	$ 3,245	$ 3,956 ($17,529 x 0.2257)	$ 4,823 ($21,368 x 0.2257)	$ 5,879 ($26,048 x 0.2257)	$ 7,167 ($31,753 x 0.2257)
NOA***	$19,960	$24,346 ($17,529 / 0.72)	$29,678 ($21,368 / 0.72)	$36,178 ($26,048 / 0.72)	$44,101 ($31,753 / 0.72)

   *   Sales = Prior year sales x (1+ Growth of 21.90%)
   ** NOPAT = Sales x NOPM (22.57%)
   *** NOA = Sales / NOAT (0.72)

PROBLEMS

P11-32 (60 minutes)

We forecast Intuit, Inc. using the following forecast assumptions

Revenue growth	14.9%
Cost of revenue...	18.6%
Selling and marketing / Total net revenue...........................	28.4%
Research and development / Total net revenue	17.0%
General and administrative / Total net revenue....................	11.5%
Acquisition related charges / Total net revenue...................	0.6%
Income tax provision/Income before tax	38.0%
Depreciation / Total net revenue (Depreciation included in G&A) ...	4.0%
Sales/Year-end accounts receivable....................................	23.90
Sales / Year-end property and equipment, net	12.07
Sales/ Year-end accounts payable.......................................	32.99
Sales /Year-end accrued compensation...............................	13.62

We assume that growth, expense percentages and turnover rates from the previous year, will continue. We estimated one growth rate for combined revenue. A refinement would be to estimate separate growth rates. We also estimated one gross profit ratio. Again, we could have refined the analysis by estimating one profit ratio for each type of revenue. Because Intuit's "cost of sales" line item is not directly related to payables (cost of sales are mostly employee salaries etc), we calculate the AP turnover ratio using sales. We assume other accounts not listed above will remain constant. Your assumptions may, of course, differ from ours, and these differences will lead to different forecasted financial statements. Based on our assumptions, we estimate Intuit's income statement, balance sheet, and statement of cash flows as follows:

P11-32—continued.

Intuit, Inc., Income Statement

($ millions)							2007
Total net revenue	(	$2,342	x	1.149	)	$	2,691
Cost of revenues.....................................	(	$2,691	x	0.186	)		501
Gross profit	(	$2,691	x	0.814	)		2,190
Selling and marketing............................	(	$2,691	x	28.4%	)		764
Research and development	(	$2,691	x	17.0%	)		457
General and administrative..................	(	$2,691	x	11.5%	)		309
Acquisition related charges..................	(	$2,691	x	0.6%	)		16
Operating income							643
Interest and other expense (income) ..	(	no change			)		50
Income before tax							693
Income tax provision.............................	(	$693	x	38.0%	)		263
Minority interest expense	(	no change			)		(1)
Net income...						$	429

Intuit, Inc., Balance Sheet

($ millions)							2007
Cash and equivalents	(	computed	*		)	$	601
Investments	(	no change			)		1,018
Accounts receivable	(	$2,691	/	23.90	)		113
Deferred tax assets	(	no change			)		47
Deferred income tax, prepaid expenses and other, and funds held for payroll customers	(	no change			)		474
Total Current Assets							2,253
Property and equipment, net	(	$2,691	/	12.07	)		223
Goodwill and other assets	(	no change			)		759
Total Assets						$	3,235
Accounts Payable	(	$2,691	/	32.99	)	$	82
Accrued compensation and related liabilities	(	$2,691	/	13.62	)		198
Deferred revenue	(	no change			)		293
Other current liabilities and payroll customer fund deposits	(	no change			)		480
Total Current Liabilities							1,052
Long-term obligations	(	no change			)		15
Total liabilities							1,067
Common Stock and additional paid-in capital	(	no change			)		2,094
Treasury stock	(	no change			)		(1,944)
Deferred compensation	(	no change			)		0
Accumulated other comprehensive income	(	no change			)		1
Retained earnings	(	computed	**		)		2,017
Stockholders' Equity							2,168
Total Liabilities and Equity						$	3,235

* Total assets less non-cash assets
** Beginning Retained earnings $1,588 + Net income $429 - Dividends $0

P11-32—(continued)

Intuit, Inc., Statement of Cash Flows

($ millions)					2007
Operating activities					
Net income... (	from above			) $	429
Depreciation .... (	$2,691	x	4.0%	)	108
Accounts receivables............................ (	$98	-	$113	)	(15)
Accounts Payable.................................. (	$82	-	$71	)	11
Accrued compensation .... (	$198	-	$172	)	26
Net cash flows from operating activities..					558
Investing activities					
Investment in PPE (net)***					(137)
Net cash flow from investing activities...					(137)
Financing activities					
Net cash flows from financing activities...					0
Net change in cash					421
Beginning cash					180
Ending cash...				$	601

*** Beginning PPE $194 – Ending PPE $223 – Depreciation $108

Our forecasts indicate that Intuit will not require financing in fiscal 2007. Its projected cash balance is $601 million, 18.6% of total assets, which is far in excess of the 6.5% of total assets is reported in the prior year. The excess cash can be invested in marketable securities as a store of liquidity, or it can be used to retire debt and/or repurchase stock. We did not modify our forecasted numbers for this extra cash.

P11-34 (40 minutes)

There are a number of line items that should be considered as possible adjustments to the income statements for Xerox over the past three years:

a. *Restructuring and impairment costs.* These costs involve a significant level of estimates (timing and amount of potential asset impairment or expected costs of employee severance). Consequently, we need to carefully read and dissect the discussion of these costs in the MD&A. The company's past accuracy in estimating these types of costs might also affect the degree to which we might question these costs. In addition, companies can control not only the amount or reported asset impairment, but also when the impairment is recognized. As a result, we need to review management's discussion of these charges in the MD&A section.

b. *Gain on affiliate's sale of stock.* This is the gain recognized by the parent when its subsidiary sells previously unissued stock to the investing public. It is a transitory item.

c. *Equity in income of unconsolidated affiliates.* This accrual relates to Xerox' proportionate share of the net income of companies that Xerox accounts for using the equity method. This is typically a continuing item unless the investment in the affiliate is sold. This is also typically an operating item.

d. *Income from discontinued operations.* This is a transitory item and relates to the operating profit (loss) and gain (loss) on the sale of a business unit that is offered for sale or has been sold in the current year.

e. *Cumulative effect of change in accounting principle.* Under prior GAAP (in effect in the year of this income statement), companies reported the cumulative effect, net of tax, of changes in accounting principles "below the line," that is, below income from continuing operations. These items are all transitory. Under current GAAP, these effects are applied retrospectively to all years presented with an adjustment to the opening balance of retained earnings for the earliest year.

Module 12

Analyzing and Valuing Equity Securities

QUESTIONS

Q12-2. The DCF and ROPI models define the price of a security in terms of the company's expected free cash flow to the firm (FCFF) and the expected residual operating income (ROPI), respectively. These expectations are, then, discounted to the present, using the WACC as the discount rate, to calculate an estimated share price. Expectations about the future financial performance of a company, therefore, influence significantly expected market value. There is an inverse relation between securities prices and expected return, the discount rate (WACC in this case).

Q12-4. The "weighted average cost of capital" captures the average cost of funds that the firm has raised from both debt and equity sources, weighted by the proportion received from each financing source. The cost of debt is measured as the after-tax interest rate. The cost of equity is the expected return required by equity investors, usually approximated using the Capital Asset Pricing Model (CAPM) which posits the expected return as a function of the risk free rate, the company's beta (the historic variability of its stock returns), and the "spread" of equity securities over the risk free rate.

Q12-6. Net operating assets are equal to total operating assets less total operating liabilities. Typically excluded are nonoperating assets such as investments in marketable securities, non-strategic equity investments (but not equity method investments made for strategic purposes), net assets of discontinued operations, and nonoperating liabilities such as interest-bearing debt and capitalized lease obligations.

Q12-8. Disaggregating RNOA into its component parts (as the ROPI model does) highlights that the value of a firm depends critically on both turnover and profit margin. Company value will be increased if managers can increase NOPAT while holding NOA constant, and/or if managers can reduce NOA while holding NOPAT constant. Holding sales constant, NOPAT increases with NOPM, and NOA decreases with NOAT. NOPM and NOAT, then, must *both* be managed well for a company to increase ROPI and therefore, increase stock price.

MINI EXERCISES

M12-10 (10 minutes)

$3,305 million – (6.66% x $12,972 million) = $2,441 million.

M12-12 (15 minutes)

a. PepsiCo earned a positive ROPI in 2005 because realized NOPAT exceeds the *expected* NOPAT (given the cost of capital and the beginning NOA). $4,140 million – (5.78% x $18,908 million) = $3,047 million.

b. PepsiCo will earn a positive ROPI up to a WACC of 21.9%. At this level of WACC, ROPI = ($18,908 million) x 21.9% = $4,140, the level of NOPAT.

EXERCISES

E12-14 (30 minutes)
a.

ANF ($millions)	Current 2006	Forecast Horizon 2007	2008	2009	2010	Terminal Year
Sales	$2,785	$3,838	$5,289	$7,288	$10,043	$10,244
NOPAT	325	448	617	851	1,172	1,195
NOA	616	849	1,170	1,612	2,222	2,266
DCF Model						
Increase in NOA		233	321	442	610	44
FCFF (NOPAT - Increase in NOA)		215	296	409	562	1,151
Discount factor [1 / (1 × r_w)^t]		0.88496	0.78315	0.69305	0.61332	
Present value of horizon FCFF		190	232	283	345	
Cum present value of horizon FCFF	$1,050					
Present value of terminal FCFF	6,418					
Total firm value	7,468					
Less NNO (Plus negative NNO)	(379)					
Firm equity value	$7,847					
Shares outstanding (millions)	103.3					
Stock price per share	$75.96					
ROPI Model						
ROPI (NOPAT - [NOA_{Beg} × r_w])		$ 368	$ 507	$ 699	$ 962	$ 906
Discount factor [1 / (1 × r_w)^t]		0.88496	0.78315	0.69305	0.61332	
Present value of horizon ROPI		326	397	484	590	
Cum present value of horizon ROPI	$1,797					
Present value of terminal ROPI	5,052					
NOA	616					
Total firm value	$7,465					
Less NNO (Plus negative NNO)	(379)					
Firm equity value	7,844					
Shares outstanding (millions)	103.3					
Stock value per share	$ 75.93	($0.03 difference due to rounding)				

E12-14—continued

b. Our stock price estimate or $75.93 is higher than the ANF market price of $66.39 as of 1/31/06, indicating that we believe that ANF stock is undervalued. Stock prices are a function of expected NOPAT and NOA, as well as the WACC discount rate. Our higher stock price estimate may be due to more optimistic forecasts or a lower discount rate compared to other investors' and analysts' model assumptions. If, after further analysis, we are convinced that the stock is indeed undervalued, we could take a long position in ANF. By late 2006, ANF stock was trading at over $75 per share—see ANF's one-year stock price chart below for 2006.

E12-16 (20 minutes)

($millions)

a. NOA = $20,513 − $272 − $1,256 − $469 − $989 − $1,452 − $3,866
         = $12,209
    NNO = $1,072 + $1,309 − $272
         = $2,109

b. $12,209 = $2,109 + $10,100
    (NOA) = (NNO) +   (SE)

E12-18 (30 minutes)

a.

3M ($millions)	Current 2005	Forecast Horizon				Terminal Year
		2006	2007	2008	2009	
Sales................................	$21,167	$22,395	$23,694	$25,068	$26,522	$26,787
NOPAT...............................	3,306	3,498	3,701	3,916	4,143	4,184
NOA..................................	12,209	12,945	13,696	14,490	15,331	15,484

DCF Model

Increase in NOA		$ 736	$ 751	$ 794	$ 841	$ 153
FCFF (NOPAT - Increase in NOA) ..		2,762	2,950	3,122	3,302	4,031
Discount factor $[1 / (1 \times r_w)^t]$		0.93458	0.87344	0.81630	0.76290	
Present value of horizon FCFF		2,581	2,577	2,548	2,519	
Cum present value of horizon FCFF	$10,225					
Present value of terminal FCFF.......	51,254					
Total firm value	61,479					
Less NNO.......................................	2,109					
Firm equity value	$59,370					
Shares outstanding (millions)	754.5					
Stock price per share......................	$ 78.69					

ROPI Model

ROPI (NOPAT = $[NOA_{Beg} \times r_w]$)		$ 2,643	$ 2,795	$ 2,957	$ 3,129	$ 3,111
Discount factor $[1 / (1 \times r_w)^t]$		0.93458	0.87344	0.81630	0.76290	
Present value of horizon ROPI........		2,470	2,441	2,414	2,387	
Cum present value of horizon ROPI	$ 9,712					
Present value of terminal ROPI.......	39,556					
NOA..	12,209					
Total firm value	61,477					
Less NNO.......................................	2,109					
Firm equity value	$59,368					
Shares outstanding (millions)	754.5					
Stock value per share......................	$ 78.69					

b. Our stock price estimate of $78.69 is slightly higher than the MMM market price of $78.29 as of 12/29/05, indicating that we believe that the stock is slightly undervalued. Stock prices are a function of expected NOPAT and NOA, as well as the WACC discount rate. Our higher stock price estimate may be due to more optimistic forecasts or a lower discount rate compared to other investors' and analysts' model assumptions. By late 2006, 3M stock was trading at about $78 per share—see 3M's one-year stock price chart below for 2006.

E12-20 (15 minutes)

a. The ROPI model focuses on NOA and ROPI, where ROPI = NOPAT − (WACC x NOA_{Beg}). The components of ROPI, then, are the same components used in the computation of RNOA. The components of RNOA, profit margin (NOPM) and turnover (NOAT), are, therefore, called "value drivers" since they determine the value of the company according to this model.

b. Managers must manage *both* the income statement and the balance sheet if they are to achieve high performance. This is the valuable insight that the ROPI model highlights.

PROBLEMS

P12-22 (60 minutes)

a. 2006 NOA = $(29,029 − 946 − 268 − 810 − 1,172 − 412 − 2,830 − 1,279 − 564 − 273 − 114 − 401) million = $19,960 million.

b. 2006 NOPAT = $(4,736 − (1,429 − ((170 + 25 + 48 − 169) × 0.364)) million = $3,334 million

c.

ORCL ($millions)	Current 2006	Forecast Horizon 2007	2008	2009	2010	Terminal Year
Sales	$14,380	$17,529	$21,368	$26,048	$31,752	$32,387
NOPAT	3,334	4,065	4,955	6,041	7,363	7,511
NOA	19,960	24,346	29,678	36,178	44,100	44,982

d.

ORCL ($millions)	Current 2006	Forecast Horizon 2007	2008	2009	2010	Terminal Year
DCF Model						
Increase in NOA		$4,386	$5,332	$6,500	$7,922	$ 882
FCFF (NOPAT - Increase in NOA)		(321)	(377)	(459)	(559)	6,629
Discount factor $[1 / (1 \times r_w)^t]$		0.92593	0.85734	0.79383	0.73503	
Present value of horizon FCFF		(297)	(323)	(364)	(441)	
Cum present value of horizon FCFF	$ (1,395)					
Present value of terminal FCFF	81,209					
Total firm value	79,814					
Less NNO	4,948					
Firm equity value	$ 74,866					
Shares outstanding (millions)	5,232.0					
Stock price per share	$ 14.31					
ROPI Model						
ROPI (NOPAT = $[NOA_{Beg} \times r_w]$)		$2,468	$3,007	$3,667	$4,469	$3,983
Discount factor $[1 / (1 \times r_w)^t]$		0.92593	0.85734	0.79383	0.73503	
Present value of horizon ROPI		2,285	2,578	2,911	3,285	
Cum present value of horizon ROPI	$11,059					
Present value of terminal ROPI	48794					
NOA	19,960					
Total firm value	79,813					
Less NNO	4,948					
Firm equity value	$74,865					
Shares outstanding (millions)	5,232.0					
Stock value per share	$ 14.31					

P12-22—continued

e. Our stock price estimate of $14.31 is a bit higher than the actual ORCL market price of $14.22 as of 5/31/06, indicating that we believe that Oracle's stock is just slightly undervalued. Stock prices are a function of expected NOPAT and NOA, as well as the WACC discount rate. Differences in stock price estimates may be due to more optimistic or pessimistic forecasts or a higher or lower discount rate compared to other investors' and analysts' model assumptions. If, after further analysis, we are convinced that the stock is fairly priced, we could avoid taking a long position in ORCL. By late 2006, spending the first half of the year below $15 per share, ORCL stock was trading in the $18 per share range—see ORCL's one-year stock price chart below for 2006. Perhaps new information came to the market in mid-year that caused estimates to be more optimistic than the information we used at the beginning of the year.

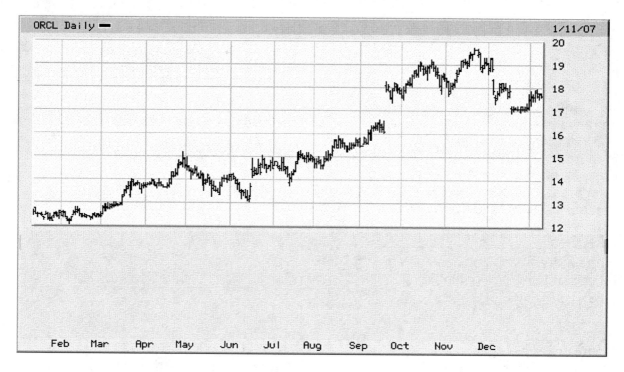

P12-24 (60 minutes)

a. NOA ($ 000s) = Operating assets – Operating liabilities
  ($5,255,209 – $905,197) –
  ([$873,112 – $204,973] + $155,236 + $60,975 + $82,281)
  = $3,383,381

b. NOPAT ($ 000s) = $1,487,759 – $22,797 – ($528,155 – [$22,797 x 37.3%])
  = $945,310

c.

HOG ($ millions)	Current 2005	Forecast Horizon 2006	2007	2008	2009	Terminal Year
Sales	$5,342	$5,689	$6,059	$6,453	$6,872	$7,010
NOPAT	945	1,007	1,072	1,142	1,216	1,241
NOA	3,383	3,601	3,835	4,084	4,349	4,437

d.

HOG ($ millions)	Current 2005	Forecast Horizon 2006	2007	2008	2009	Terminal Year
DCF Model						
Increase in NOA		$ 218	$ 234	$ 249	$ 265	$ 88
FCFF (NOPAT - Increase in NOA)		789	838	893	951	1,153
Discount factor [$1 / (1 \times r_w)^t$]		0.93458	0.87344	0.81630	0.76290	
Present value of horizon FCFF		737	732	729	726	
Cum present value of horizon FCFF	$ 2,924					
Present value of terminal FCFF	17,592					
Total firm value	20,516					
Less NNO	299					
Firm equity value	$20,217					
Shares outstanding (millions)	274					
Stock value per share	$ 73.78					
ROPI Model						
ROPI (NOPAT - [$NOA_{Beg} \times r_w$])		$ 770	$ 820	$ 874	$ 930	$ 937
Discount factor [$1 / (1 \times r_w)^t$]		0.93458	0.87344	0.81630	0.76290	
Present value of horizon ROPI		720	716	713	709	
Cum present value of horizon ROPI	$ 2,858					
Present value of terminal ROPI	14,297					
NOA	3,383					
Total firm value	20,538					
Less NNO	299					
Firm equity value	$20,239					
Shares outstanding (millions)	274					
Stock value per share	$ 73.86					

($0.08 difference due to rounding)

©Cambridge Business Publishers, 2008

P12-24—continued

e. Our stock price estimate of $73.85 is higher than the HOG market price of $51.49 as of 12/30/2005, indicating that we believe that the stock is undervalued. Stock prices are a function of expected NOPAT and NOA, as well as the WACC discount rate. Our higher stock price estimate might be due to more optimistic forecasts or a lower discount rate compared to other investors' and analysts' model assumptions. If, after further analysis, we are convinced that the stock is indeed undervalued, we could take a long position in HOG. By late 2006, HOG stock was trading in the $74 per share range—see HOG's one-year stock price chart below for 2006.

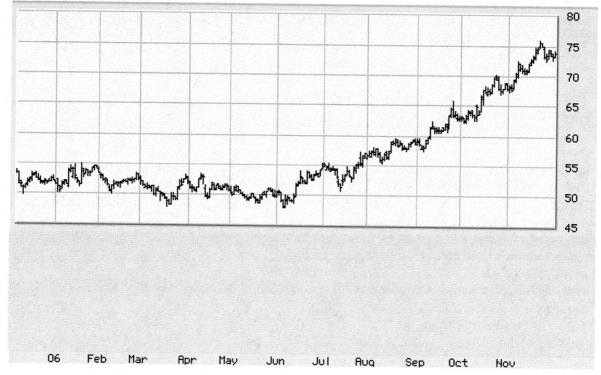

Financial Accounting for MBAs, 3rd Edition

Appendix B

Constructing the Statement of Cash Flows

QUESTIONS

Q B-2 Cash equivalents are included with cash in a statement of cash flows because the purchase and sale of such investments are considered to be part of a firm's overall management of cash rather than a source or use of cash. Similarly, as statement users evaluate cash flows, it may matter very little to them whether the cash is on hand, deposited in a bank account, or invested in cash equivalents.

Q B-4 a. Investing; outflow.
  b. Investing; inflow.
  c. Financing; outflow.
  d. Operating (direct method, not shown separately under indirect method); inflow.
  e. Financing; inflow.
  f. Operating (direct method, not shown separately under indirect method); inflow.
  g. Operating (direct method, shown as supplemental information under indirect method); outflow.
  h. Operating (direct method, not shown separately under indirect method); inflow.

Q B-6 Noncash investing and financing transactions are disclosed as supplemental information to a statement of cash flows because a secondary objective of cash flow reporting is to present information about investing and financing activities. Noncash investing and financing transactions generally affect future cash flows. Issuing bonds payable to acquire equipment, for example, requires future cash payments for interest and principal on the bonds. On the other hand, converting bonds payable into common stock eliminates future cash payments related to the bonds. Knowledge of these types of events, therefore, should be helpful to users of cash flow data who wish to assess a firm's future cash flows.

Q B-8[B1] The direct method presents the net cash flow from operating activities by showing the major categories of operating cash receipts and cash payments (such as cash received from customers, cash paid to employees and suppliers, cash paid for interest, and cash paid for income taxes). The indirect (or *reconciliation*) method, in contrast, presents the net cash flow from operating activities by applying a series of adjustments to the accrual net income to convert it to a cash basis.

Q B-10 Under the indirect method, the $98,000 cash received from the sale of the land will appear in the cash flows from investing activities section of the statement of cash flows. In addition, the $28,000 gain from the sale will be deducted from net income as one of the adjustments made to determine the net cash flow from operating activities.

Q B-12 The separate disclosures required for a company using the indirect method in the statement of cash flows are (1) cash paid during the year for interest (net of amount capitalized) and for income taxes, (2) all noncash investing and financing transactions, and (3) the policy for determining which highly liquid, short-term investments are treated as cash equivalents.

Q B-14[B1]

Sales	$925,000
+ Accounts receivable decrease	14,000
= Cash received from customers	$939,000

Q B-16[B1]

Advertising expense	$43,000
+ Prepaid advertising increase	1,600
= Cash paid for advertising	$44,600

Q B-18[B1] The separate disclosures required for a company using the direct method in the statement of cash flows are (1) a reconciliation of net income to net cash flow from operating activities, (2) all noncash investing and financing transactions, and (3) the policy for determining which highly liquid, short-term investments are treated as cash equivalents.

Q B-20 The operating cash flow to capital expenditures ratio is calculated by dividing a firm's cash flow from operating activities by its annual capital expenditures. A ratio below 1.00 means that the firm's current operating activities do not provide enough cash to cover the capital expenditures. A ratio above 1.0 is normally considered a sign of financial strength.

MINI EXERCISES

M B-22 (10 minutes)

a.   Cash inflow from an operating activity.
b.   Cash inflow from an investing activity.
c.   Cash outflow from an investing activity.
d.   Cash outflow from an operating activity.
e.   Cash inflow from a financing activity.
f.   Cash outflow from a financing activity.
g.   Cash outflow from an investing activity.

M B-24 (15 minutes—INDIRECT METHOD)

Net Income	$ 45,000
Add (Deduct) Items to Convert Net Income to Cash Basis	
Depreciation	8,000
Gain on Sale of Investments	(9,000)
Accounts Receivable Increase	(9,000)
Inventory Increase	(6,000)
Prepaid Rent Decrease	2,000
Accounts Payable Increase	4,000
Income Tax Payable Decrease	(2,000)
Net Cash Provided by Operating Activities	$ 33,000

M B-26 (15 minutes—DIRECT METHOD)

a.	Rent Expense	$ 60,000
	− Prepaid Rent Decrease	(2,000)
	= Cash Paid for Rent	$ 58,000
b.	Interest Income	$ 16,000
	− Interest Receivable Increase	(700)
	= Cash Received as Interest	$ 15,300
c.	Cost of Goods Sold	$ 98,000
	+ Inventory Increase	3,000
	+ Accounts Payable Decrease	4,000
	= Cash Paid for Merchandise Purchased	$105,000

EXERCISES

E B-28 (15 minutes—INDIRECT METHOD)

Net Income	$113,000
Add (Deduct) Items to Convert Net Income to Cash Basis	
Accounts Receivable Increase	(5,000)
Inventory Decrease	6,000
Prepaid Insurance Increase	(1,000)
Accounts Payable Increase	4,000
Wages Payable Decrease	(2,000)
Net Cash Provided by Operating Activities	$115,000

E B-30[B1] (20 minutes—DIRECT METHOD)

a.	Advertising expense	$ 62,000
+	Prepaid advertising increase	4,000
=	Cash paid for advertising	$ 66,000
b.	Income tax expense	$ 29,000
+	Income tax payable decrease	2,200
=	Cash paid for income taxes	$ 31,200
c.	Cost of goods sold	$180,000
–	Inventory decrease	(5,000)
–	Accounts payable increase	(2,000)
=	Cash paid for merchandise purchased	$173,000

E B-32^{B1} (30 minutes—DIRECT METHOD)

	Sales	$750,000
−	Accounts Receivable Increase	(5,000)
=	Cash Received from Customers	$745,000
	Cost of Goods Sold	$470,000
−	Inventory Decrease	(6,000)
−	Accounts Payable Increase	(4,000)
=	Cash Paid for Merchandise Purchased	$460,000
	Wages Expense	$110,000
+	Wages Payable Decrease	2,000
=	Cash Paid to Employees	$112,000
	Insurance Expense	$ 15,000
+	Prepaid Insurance Increase	1,000
=	Cash Paid for Insurance	$ 16,000

Operating Activities

Cash Received from Customers		$745,000
Cash Paid for Merchandise Purchased	$460,000	
Cash Paid to Employees	112,000	
Cash Paid for Rent	42,000	
Cash Paid for Insurance	16,000	630,000
Net Cash Provided by Operating Activities		$115,000

PROBLEMS

P B-34 (45 minutes—Indirect Method)

a.
Cash, December 31, 2007	$11,000
Cash, December 31, 2006	5,000
Cash increase during 2007	$ 6,000

b. (Indirect Method)

WOLFF COMPANY
STATEMENT OF CASH FLOWS
FOR YEAR ENDED DECEMBER 31, 2007

Net Cash Flow from Operating Activities		
Net Income		$56,000
Add (Deduct) Items to Convert Net Income to Cash Basis		
Depreciation	17,000	
Accounts Receivable Increase	(9,000)	
Inventory Increase	(30,000)	
Prepaid Insurance Decrease	2,000	
Accounts Payable Decrease	(3,000)	
Wages Payable Increase	3,000	
Income Tax Payable Decrease	(1,000)	
Net Cash Provided by Operating Activities		$35,000
Cash Flows from Investing Activities		
Purchase of Plant Assets		(55,000)
Cash Flows from Financing Activities		
Issuance of Bonds Payable	55,000	
Payment of Dividends	(29,000)	
Net Cash Provided by Financing Activities		26,000
Net Increase in Cash		6,000
Cash at Beginning of Year		5,000
Cash at End of Year		$11,000

P B-36 (50 minutes—INDIRECT METHOD)

a.
Cash, December 31, 2007	$27,000
Cash, December 31, 2006	18,000
Cash increase during 2007	$ 9,000

b. (INDIRECT METHOD)

DAIR COMPANY
STATEMENT OF CASH FLOWS
FOR YEAR ENDED DECEMBER 31, 2007

Net Cash Flow from Operating Activities		
Net Income	$ 85,000	
Add (Deduct) Items to Convert Net Income to Cash Basis		
Depreciation	22,000	
Goodwill Amortization	7,000	
Loss on Bond Retirement	5,000	
Accounts Receivable Increase	(5,000)	
Inventory Decrease	6,000	
Prepaid Expenses Increase	(2,000)	
Accounts Payable Increase	6,000	
Interest Payable Decrease	(3,000)	
Income Tax Payable Decrease	(2,000)	
Net Cash Provided by Operating Activities		119,000
Cash Flows from Investing Activities		
Sale of Equipment		17,000
Cash Flows from Financing Activities		
Retirement of Bonds Payable	(125,000)	
Issuance of Common Stock	24,000	
Payment of Dividends	(26,000)	
Net Cash Used by Financing Activities		(127,000)
Net Increase in Cash		9,000
Cash at Beginning of Year		18,000
Cash at End of Year		$ 27,000

P B-36—continued

c.

(1)   **Supplemental Cash Flow Disclosures**
        Cash Paid for Interest.. **$ 13,000***
        Cash Paid for Income Taxes.. **$ 38,000†**

     *   Interest expense.. $10,000
      + Interest payable decrease 3,000
        Cash paid for interest $13,000

     †   Income tax expense... $36,000
      + Income tax payable decrease 2,000
        Cash paid for income taxes $38,000

(2)   **Schedule of Noncash Investing and Financing Activities**
        Issuance of Bonds Payable to Acquire Equipment .... **$ 60,000**

P B-38 (35 minutes—DIRECT METHOD)

a. Cash, December 31, 2007 .... $11,000
   Cash, December 31, 2006 5,000
   Cash increase during 2007 .... $ 6,000

b.

Wolff COMPANY
STATEMENT OF CASH FLOWS
FOR YEAR ENDED DECEMBER 31, 2007

Cash Flows from Operating Activities

Cash Received from Customers		$626,000
Cash Paid for Merchandise Purchased	$ 463,000	
Cash Paid to Employees	83,000	
Cash Paid for Insurance	6,000	
Cash Paid for Interest	9,000	
Cash Paid for Income Taxes	30,000	591,000
Net Cash Provided by Operating Activities		35,000
Cash Flows from Investing Activities		
Purchase of Plant Assets		(55,000)
Cash Flows from Financing Activities		
Issuance of Bonds Payable	55,000	
Payment of Dividends	(29,000)	
Net Cash Provided by Financing Activities		26,000
Net Increase in Cash		6,000
Cash at Beginning of Year		5,000
Cash at End of Year		$ 11,000

P B-40[B1] (60 minutes—DIRECT METHOD)

a.
Cash, December 31, 2007	$27,000
Cash, December 31, 2006	18,000
Cash increase during 2007	$ 9,000

b.

DAIR COMPANY
STATEMENT OF CASH FLOWS
FOR YEAR ENDED DECEMBER 31, 2007

Cash Flows from Operating Activities

Cash Received from Customers		$695,000
Cash Paid for Merchandise Purchased	$428,000	
Cash Paid for Wages and Other Operating Expenses	97,000	
Cash Paid for Interest	13,000	
Cash Paid for Income Taxes	38,000	(576,000)
Net Cash Provided by Operating Activities		119,000

Cash Flows from Investing Activities

Sale of Equipment		17,000

Cash Flows from Financing Activities

Retirement of Bonds Payable	(125,000)	
Issuance of Common Stock	24,000	
Payment of Dividends	(26,000)	
Net Cash Used by Financing Activities		(127,000)

Net Increase in Cash	9,000
Cash at Beginning of Year	18,000
Cash at End of Year	$ 27,000

P B-40—continued

c.

(1) Reconciliation of Net Income to Net Cash Flow from Operating Activities

Operating Activities	
Net Income	$ 85,000
Add (Deduct) Items to Convert Net Income to Cash Basis	
Depreciation	22,000
Goodwill Amortization	7,000
Loss on Bond Retirement	5,000
Accounts Receivable Increase	(5,000)
Inventory Decrease	6,000
Prepaid Expenses Increase	(2,000)
Accounts Payable Increase	6,000
Interest Payable Decrease	(3,000)
Income Tax Payable Decrease	(2,000)
Net Cash Provided by Operating Activities	$119,000

(2) Schedule of Noncash Investing and Financing Activities

Issuance of Bonds Payable to Acquire Equipment	$ 60,000

P B-42 (45 minutes)

a. Depreciation is a noncash expense that is deducted in the computation of net income. The depreciation add-back zeros this expense out of the income statement to focus on cash profitability. The positive amount for depreciation does not mean that the company is generating cash from depreciation, a common misconception. It is merely an adjustment to remove that expense from the computation of profit.

b. Cash inflows relating to the tax benefits realized when employees exercise stock options are not a reliable source of funds as the exercise will only take place when the purchase price of the stock exceeds the exercise (strike) price of the option. In fact, many companies realized a reduction in operating cash flows during the bear market of the early 2000s as a result of this very occurrence.

c. The negative sign indicates an *outflow* of cash. This arises because receivables have *increased* during the period.

d. The positive sign indicates an *inflow* of cash. Accrued liabilities arise as a result of an entry made on the accounting records by the company for which there has not been a corresponding cash transaction. An example is the accrual of wages earned by employees during the period that will be paid in a subsequent period. The positive amount indicates an inflow of cash as a result of the increase in accrued liabilities. The company's operating cash flows have increased as a result of delaying payment of amounts due. These liabilities must be paid in the future, however, and the payment will result in a reduction in operating cash flow as evidenced by the reduction in accrued liabilities. Unless accrued liabilities are expected to remain at the current higher level, the current period increase in cash flow is only temporary and will reverse at a later period when the liabilities return to a lower level.

e. During 2007, Amgen generated $3,566.6 million in cash flows from operating activities. It used $3,210.2 million for investing activities, primarily to purchase property, plant and equipment (PPE) to grow its infrastructure and to increase marketable securities that provide a significant source of liquidity for the company. The company also used $1,371.5 million for financing activities, primarily relating to the repurchase of common stock. In sum, the cash flow picture of the company is healthy. It is generating significant operating cash flows and is using that source of funds to grow the infrastructure (PPE) of the business, with the excess used to acquire common stock or accumulated in marketable securities.